**Changing Course: Stories to Navigate Career and Life Transitions**

Copyright © 2016 by Shelaine Strom

Published in Abbotsford, BC by In the Midst Publishing

All rights reserved. No part of this publication may be reproduced, stored in a retrieval system, or transmitted in any form by any means, electronic, mechanical, photocopy, recording or otherwise without the prior written permission of the publisher, except as provided for by Canadian copyright law.

Cover Design: Brittany Martin

Layout: Brittany Martin

First Printing: 2016

Paperback ISBN: 978-0-9951505-0-8

EBook ISBN: 978-0-9951505-1-5

For William

My mutual edit-fication partner

# Table of Contents

| | |
|---|---|
| Introduction | 1 |
| **Why is Change Happening to Me?** | |
|     Jimmy the Hamster | 5 |
|     Feeling Cast Away | 10 |
| **Who Am I in This Journey?** | |
|     Personality 101 | 17 |
|     You've Got Style | 23 |
| **Why Isn't Showing Up Enough?** | |
|     "Hello-oo!" | 38 |
|     End Well | 43 |
|     Wish List | 49 |
| **Who Cares?** | |
|     Betty's Story | 57 |
|     Perils of Instructing | 63 |
| **Can't You Just Hire Me?** | |
|     "I Hate Animals!" | 71 |
|     A Bikini and a Little Black Dress | 79 |
|     The Wordless Interview | 87 |
| **What Should I Be When I Grow Up?** | |
|     The Chaos Theory of Squirrels | 92 |
|     Grandpa's Scree Sifter | 100 |
| **How Do I Juggle All My Lives?** | |
|     Drawing the Line | 107 |
|     Rocks, Pebbles and Sand | 115 |
| **I Have to Work With These People?** | |
|     Hooked | 126 |
|     Lunch Anyone? | 131 |
|     Belligerent | 136 |

| | |
|---|---|
| Where is the "I" in Team? | |
|     To the Moon | 145 |
|     Building Mania | 152 |
| Where Do I Go Now? | |
|     Open Hand, Closed Hand | 162 |
|     Zig-Zag | 167 |
| Conclusion | 173 |
| Notes | 176 |

# Acknowledgements

My heartfelt gratitude to all of you who read the early drafts of this manuscript and cared enough to interact with the content – Rosabelle Birch, Karen Stobbe, Joan Bird, Barb McLachlan, Lisa Unrau, Jaydene Hefferland, Cheryl Heffner, Wendy Toews, Jean Strom, Sue Braid, Bev Montgomery, and Joey Demers. It's a better read because of your comments.

Hugs to my sons – Taylor, Clark and Eric – for providing me with so many stories – and permission to tell them.

A special thank you to Dr. Roberta Neault for making time during your world travels to engage with me on this project.

Loranne Brown, you said I could write and encouraged me to do so. A million thanks.

And to my husband, Bill, for the countless hours we spent in front of the fire reworking sentences and brainstorming words. Thanks for being my biggest fan and honest critic. I use far fewer sentence fragments because of you.

# Introduction

When life takes an immediate left where you expected a right, what follows is akin to chaos. It feels like everything known, isn't; routine is replaced by random; the bedrock of your identity quakes; adventure adrenaline soars, thrilling some and crippling others. There is no straight line through transition.

I have spent two decades as a career instructor and coach walking alongside people in such throes of job loss. I originally stumbled into the field and spent early years feeling like an imposter who needed to do things right and cover material by the book. It took angry clients, the uncooperative, the broken, and the appreciative to challenge my thinking and clarify my role.

I learned that getting facts and theory right matters far less to people than I imagined. I taught the content and, more importantly, felt I genuinely cared for clients (though not easily or perfectly). I attempted to treat each person with respect and dignity, affirming their value by listening to their unique story. Feedback I received consistently confirmed that people valued being cared for and heard as much or more than learning concepts and tools.

## CHANGING COURSE

So gradually I left behind the façade of answers and became a seed planter. I tilled the soil through empathy, created a safe place, and offered kernels of opportunity to learn. What roots took, the watering each one received, and how growth transpired beyond the classroom has rarely been mine to know. I simply did my part and let go of the outcome.

More recently changing course has become personal. In the spring of 2012 this dream course – the one that brought twelve new people across my path each month providing opportunity to journey with the resilient and downtrodden – ended abruptly when the contract was up and not renewed.

No longer in my life were the people who pushed my buttons, delighted my heart, challenged my skills, and made each day in the classroom a cross between Pandora's Box and a treasure chest. I entered my own sojourn of change, shifting my role from coach to client.

My work ended because the contract finished, but had that not been the case, I would still have needed to be done. I had a jaw injury that required surgery for which I spent two years in pain on a wait list. Increased discomfort from talking stalled my career and sent me on a new, quieter trajectory.

In May 2014 I underwent successful replacement of my jaw joints and spent the next two years in physical rehabilitation, vocational reinventing, and writing this book.

You will find in these pages true stories of people (names changed, of course) on paths of transition and how they showed up in my world over two decades. They are a messy bunch, full of tales and antics that kept me on my toes. But that's what I loved about my work - real people doing the hard stuff of life and letting me walk with them for a short time as they changed course.

I would love to say that this book documents lives changed for greatness, but I know better than that, and mostly I just don't know if it's true. You may find yourself in these pages as I have, not only as the career coach but as the participant, the fellow journey-mate seeking to live well and find your way through whatever transitions life throws at you.

# WHY IS CHANGE HAPPENING TO ME?

# Jimmy The Hampster

Twelve sets of eyes, some brimming with anticipation, some with tears, stared at me as I walked into our classroom. Silence hung broken only by the occasional flipping of pages in new binders. I felt their eyes following me as I turned on the projector, collected my materials and took my seat in the center of the U-shaped tables.

"Welcome here. My name is Shelaine and I will be your instructor today and for several other sessions throughout this month. Today is Change Day, and I suspect that by sitting here in a job transition program you have all the proof you need that change happens." Several people smiled and nodded knowingly but a few folded their arms across their chests. I had done this long enough to know some were wondering if this course would be worth their time.

Introductions concluded, preliminary business covered, I posed the question, "Have any of you ever owned a hamster?" Some eyes rolled and others tilted their heads with an accompanying 'huh?' John appeared to be concluding that this was definitely not where he needed to be.

I explained my question with a story.

# CHANGING COURSE

"At age 12 years 11 months our middle son, Clark, informed me that he would like a hamster for his birthday. I have never owned a hamster and I've never wanted to own a hamster so the voice inside my head screamed, *There will be no rodents living in my house!* Fortunately, I managed to respond calmly, telling him that I'd think about it and talk it over with his dad. As he walked away, I secretly hoped it was just another passing phase."

Several class members smirked, knowing I was a wishful thinker as they recalled personal journeys into hamster-land. Clearly they believed I had been drawn into a losing battle.

"A week later, my son found me in the laundry room and took up his case. 'Mom, I was thinking about getting a hamster. Here's the thing. I would have to take care of him and that would teach me to be responsible.'

*Not the responsibility card*, I thought, as I felt my resolve shake. 'And,' he continued in seriousness, 'being responsible will help me be a better parent someday to your grandchildren.'"

"You're hooped!" declared Marcy from the side table.

I nodded. "We picked up the hamster on Clark's 13th birthday."

"I must confess, Jimmy, the adorable Teddy Bear hamster, won me over. He was a cute little guy and sometimes, although I'd rarely admit it, I'd even take him out of his cage and hold him when everyone was away. Jimmy and I bonded. And he taught me some important life lessons."

"He spent his days sleeping in a sawdust nest and his nights running and running on his wheel as if the whole world were on fire. His cardiovascular fitness was amazing!"

"Periodically, however, Jimmy would halt abruptly and stiffen. Head shifting to the side, eyes peering out, he would consider something beyond his steel wheel. Then, just as predictably, he resumed pace and raced his way to morning."

"Almost every day, Clark plucked Jimmy out of his world and placed him in 'the globe' – a clear, plastic ball. And without fail, each time his feet hit the plastic, Jimmy assumed his motionless statue posture. Immersed in his new circumstances, Jimmy remained frozen until his little muscles could bear the tension no longer. A leg twitched and the ball responded. Another small body movement met with a corresponding shift to the orb and before long Jimmy was racing around chairs, under tables and past stairs – blocked off for his preservation."

> "We choose the familiarity of same and known, even if it feels like a rat race."

Class participants grinned, envisioning a little fur ball whirling around furniture, dodging perils and taking in his new world.

"When we're working, we're often a lot like Jimmy. We have a routine – wake, eat, work, sleep, repeat – periodically stopping to wonder what else could exist for us, and then – for whatever our reasons – we return to the wheel again and again. We choose the familiarity of same and known, even if it feels like a rat race."

A few clients shifted in their seats, smiles faded and some broke eye contact as they began to recognize that the story wasn't just about a hamster.

"But sometimes change finds us. The equivalent of the transfer from wheel to globe happens to you or me. We find ourselves out of work or health deteriorated or relationships lost. Something changes – often not of our choosing – and we feel overwhelmed and frozen, just like Jimmy. And often we can't just pick up and move on. We need time to rest, to reflect and grieve our losses."

A man adjusted and readjusted papers in his binder. Emotion surfaced as people considered lost jobs, weeks of stunned inactivity, strained relationships and financial distress.

"But we humans tend to be resilient. Just like the little hamster whose muscles began to flinch, we can begin to take small steps to test out our new surroundings. Sometimes we find that the very scenario we figured was the worst case becomes the best case. Different worlds open up to us, new people cross our paths and we find possibilities that we couldn't have seen if we'd stayed in our wheel."

John's eyes connected with mine. "You've just described my life."

"How so?" I inquired.

"When I was twenty-one, I had just finished my bookkeeping training but my uncle offered me a job on an assembly line. It was good money so I took it and told him it was temporary, only until I found something in my field. One thing led to another, I got married, had kids, got a mortgage and twenty-eighty years later I was still working on that assembly line. I hated every day but was too scared to change. I liked the security." John leaned back and laughed cynically. "I'm just like your son's hamster!"

"Look at me now. Forty-nine years old, laid off out of the blue and no experience other than factory work." Others in the group warmed to his honesty and shared similar stories.

I added, "It's pretty safe to say that Jimmy didn't know my son's intent in moving him from spinning wheel to globe. You likely don't know the why behind the change in your life either – and you may never know for sure. Jimmy probably had little idea that his relocation could mean new worlds opening up because at first change can feel more like stripping away – raw, empty and frightening."

"So the question today is are you willing to consider that something positive, possibly even something amazing could come from the changes you're experiencing?"

John chimed in, "You know, as I'm sitting here, I'm realizing that being laid off is likely the only way I would have ever gotten out of that factory. I was too stuck in that rut to do it myself. Maybe this is a good thing…."

*"Are you willing to consider that something positive, possibly even something amazing could come from the changes you're experiencing?"*

Change, particularly when thrust upon us, can feel negative. We may focus on the losses and experience profound shifts in our routines and relationships. We can feel overwhelmed and stalled while we process all that is happening. But, like Jimmy, if we find courage to take even one small step toward embracing the new and unexpected, opportunities and growth may be the surprise we couldn't see coming.

# Feeling Cast Away

"But I wasn't fired from my job! I quit because I hated it. My supervisor constantly looked over my shoulder – I mean, stood right behind my chair and watched my screen as I did data entry. If I made a mistake, she'd point it out before I even had a chance to catch it myself. I was a nervous wreck. So, I quit."

The class members clapped for Becky's courage to do what they had only dreamed of. They looked to her to relish their support but Becky's face reflected only anger and discouragement.

"What I don't get is why I feel so awful," Becky lamented. "There were a couple of days after I walked out where I felt like the winner but then I started sinking. My work friends said they would stay in touch but they're all busy – working! I know you said people feel lost when change happens to them, but I chose this change. How come I feel lost?"

"Have you seen the movie *Castaway*?" I queried. Becky and others acknowledged that they had.

"Chuck Noland, the main character played by Tom Hanks, lived on an island for four years after his plane crashed.

He made a life of it but came to a point where his sanity depended on leaving his solitary home. Danger, uncertainty, and possibly death loomed before, but in spite of that, he built a raft and cast off shore."

"After Chuck weathered the tumultuous breakwaters surrounding the island, he began drifting out to sea. At this point in the movie, his island fades into the distance, giving him no option to go back. He turns and before him lays water. Expansive. Never-ending. Adrift on the ocean, no land in sight, alone on his floating home – all by his own choosing."

Becky looked puzzled, "So I'm supposed to be happy that I feel like Chuck, bobbing around in the middle of nowhere, all by myself?" She scanned the room for support.

"Well, probably not happy. The point is that even when we choose change, we often experience the same feelings of loss and transition as those who had change find them. And the question becomes, what are we going to do about that?" Becky shot me a skeptical look.

"Let's go back to our story for a moment. If you recall, Chuck had one friend on the island."

"W-i-l-s-o-n," shouted Jeff, sounding a great deal like the *Castaway* character.

"Yes, and he lost Wilson while he was out at sea, much like you have described the loss of work friends as a result of

> *"The point is that even when we choose change, we often experience the same feelings of loss and transition as those who had change find them."*

your decision, Becky."

I carried on. "Where the analogy breaks down is that Chuck was at the mercy of the waves and had to rely on someone to rescue him. But not you. You are not stranded and helpless. Think about this for a minute. How do ships get from one land to another?"

"They use maps and highly sophisticated, very expensive navigational equipment."

"Yes, today, they do, Jeff. And before that equipment existed they used compasses and long ago they followed the stars. Sailors use the resources available to them to set a course toward their destination – even though they can't see that new land when they leave shore – and they paddle or steam in that direction. They can trust that their movement through the marker-less waters is progress because they have an end in mind. So what navigational tools do you have for this season of few familiar signposts?"

We brainstormed together and a list of resources began to emerge: friends and family for support, research skills, websites on education opportunities, this class, other programs, self-awareness, job postings, and employment centers – the list grew and momentum built in the group.

Except for Becky. She maintained her wary frown and spoke quietly, "But I'm scared. And I feel so pathetic. Lots of people lose jobs and I feel like I can't cope with this. I sometimes wonder what's wrong with me. Why can't I just go find another job?" Others nodded, affirming her admission.

"Do you know that transition between jobs is actually a grief process?" I asked. "You've lost something and even if you hated the job, it was yours and it was a known in your life. When it ends, you experience grief over the loss – and that will be felt more intensely by some than others. Even though grieving is unique for each person, there are some common elements to the experience."

Jane spoke for the first time. "So does it include feeling like I can't get out of bed, crying over TV commercials and snapping at my kids?"

"Those are likely part of your grieving over the changes in your world. Job loss is so much more than just not working at that same place. It adds financial strain which can create relational tensions. Your time is spent differently. Other people have opinions and perhaps expectations of you. It's a very stressful time." The class nodded.

I continued. "There are some commonly agreed upon stages of grief but keep in mind, we don't progress through them in a logical, straight line. Grief is messy. The first stage in the wake of job loss is shock or denial and is characterized by numbness and disconnect from what is normal."

Jeff knew the feeling. "I couldn't believe it! I thought there had been a mistake. I was handed my box of desk contents, my pink slip and that was it. I went home and stared out the window for days, waiting for them to phone and say there had been a colossal mistake, but they never did."

"As hard as it may be to believe, that numbness is actually a protection for us. It's like entering a zone where you can't feel much because if we felt all the pain attached to our loss we couldn't stand it. So disbelief gives us time to begin slowly absorbing the pain we face.

A second stage of intense pain can emerge which involves extreme fatigue and heightened emotional symptoms as the shock wears off. It commonly includes review of circumstances prior to the loss and may contain regret, bargaining, guilt and anger. Feeling as if one is losing emotional control is one of the more frightening characteristics of this difficult yet essential phase which can take months or years, depending on the loss."

Jane grimaced, "Tell me it doesn't end with me being angry for the rest of my life."

"It doesn't have to, and this is often the point where people bump into life feeling unfair. Even when something unwanted has happened to me, I have to be the one to deal with it and make choices to move on. Think of it this way. At age fourteen, my baseball coach hit a ball that smacked me in the chin and broke my jaw. I was running out to the pitcher's mound and he didn't give warning before he hit the line drive, so when he called my name, I turned right into the full force of the hit. He didn't do it on purpose. So, who was at fault?"

> *"Will I take up a 'poor me, victim stance' or will I look at my options and take ownership of my life?"*

"The coach of course," several people volunteered.

"Let's say he is responsible. But who had to have the repair surgery, go to physiotherapy, do rehabilitation exercises and live with metal in her joints?" I asked.

"Obviously, you. And how is this good news?" Jeff posed.

"You know, it's really just the news of life. We will all face challenging circumstances at times and while we need to acknowledge and process the pain, we also get to choose how we live. Will I take up a 'poor me, victim stance' or will I look at my options and take ownership of my life? It's not an easy mix because life is hard and extremely painful at times and I get to choose how I will live in and through it. I think the good news is that I don't have to figure it all out today. All I need to do – what you can do, too – is to think about your next step. In light of this idea, what is the first, next thing you can do?"

"Keep coming to this class," Jeff suggested. "It helps me to know that I'm not the only one feeling like I do."

Jane added, "It gives me routine and I'm out of the house interacting with people. I am starting to feel normal again."

I concluded, "What you two are describing is the third stage of grief where the focus is less on what you've left behind and more on the tasks that will move you into your future. It's important to keep up supportive connections with people and remember that you will take new relationships, insights and values with you out of your loss experiences."

# WHO AM I IN THIS JOURNEY?

## Personality 101

"I'd like to begin today with each of you making a list of the characteristics in people you find difficult to work with. No names please, just write down the traits. You might put 'talks too much at work' or 'can't get a word out of him' – whatever you find challenging."

The group entered into the task quietly as was often the case on this second day of the program which focused on gaining insight into one's personality and its connection to job and career satisfaction. I watched a couple of people stare at their paper while a few madly wrote term after term. After a few more minutes I asked what made their top ten irritants and received lively replies.

Bossy people. Micromanagers. Critical or negative types. Disorganized. Late. Impatient. Don't give full instructions but expect quality results. Stubborn. Narrow minded. The terms flooded in.

"Wow, sounds like you've worked with some really difficult people!" Several agreed heartily. "Would you say that you find those qualities hard to handle because they are not like you?"

"Definitely!" replied Beth. "I had a boss who trashed anything we did. You know, like pointing out nit-picky little details. She was so critical. I'm just not like that."

"So there's an example of being not like you. Here's the harder question. If you look at your list and be brutally honest, do you struggle with characteristics in others because they are actually like you?" Silence, a few scrunched faces and squirms followed. "Whichever is the case, the goal of this session is to understand ourselves and others better. Beth, I don't know your previous boss but I wonder if it's possible that she is highly analytical and detail-oriented and it sounds like you're more big-picture or idea focused. Could it be that her approach is simply different than yours?"

Beth looked skeptical. "That would be a stretch but I guess in some ways you could say that. We are definitely different!"

"And that's really the point I'm trying to make. Different doesn't have to be a bad thing. It can just be different. But we look through our own lens and often add a judgement to it – 'if it's not the way I do it or see it or believe it, it's bad or wrong'. That's often when we end up in conflict. So today, we're looking at our personality makeup to try and see why we – and others – think and act the way we do. Ready?"

"Yes, let's do it." Jesse spoke for the crowd.

I flipped the PowerPoint to a slide identifying six personality development factors based on the Personal Style Indicator and began with discussion of bio-physical influences. "How would you say your biology has impacted your personality?" I inquired.[1]

Jesse volunteered. "Everyone in my family tells me I'm just like my uncle. I talk like him, look like him. I've even done a lot of the same kinds of work he did. It always feels weird though because he died when I was a baby so I never knew him."

"And yet people see the resemblance," I echoed. "It's true. Genetics play a significant role in who we are – like our gender or our race, for example. Other physical factors also shape us. Have any of you dealt with an ongoing health issue or injury?"

Josie nodded and spoke of a six month period off work with a herniated disc, the pain she endured and the eventual surgery.

"Josie, would you say that experience shaped your personality?"

"Totally. I have always been super independent and when this happened, I couldn't even get to the bathroom by myself. It was really hard to keep having to ask for help and to believe that people really wanted to help me. But they did. I think it made me more sensitive and I am quicker to offer help to someone else now, too."

*"Job loss or change can have a significant impact on one's self worth."*

We moved to the next slide on self-worth. "You can see here that self-worth is broken into two categories: self-concept which is how you think about yourself, your self-perception and your identity; and self-esteem is defined as the degree of acceptance and respect we have for ourselves. Job loss or change can have a significant impact on one's self worth. So, if you're feeling down on yourself right now, you're not alone."

The next slide regarding environmental systems listed family of origin, school, workplace, society, culture, geography, and climate/nature. "So how many of you would say the family you grew up in affected your personality?" I asked with a smile. "Or should I ask, who doesn't think you were affected by who you were raised around?"

"That sounds more like it," added Beth. "I'm the fifth child in a family of nine. Our house was a zoo. I could come and go and not be missed for hours. My mom used to run through the list of names until she got it right. I was likely six or seven when I realized my name wasn't John-Jerry-Lynn-Alice-Beth!" The group chuckled and Justin commented. "Wow, that's so different than my house. I'm an only child and I felt like I grew up under a microscope."

"Birth order, where we've worked, what education we've had or even the climate around us can have a profound impact on who we are today."

We moved on to another personality developmental factor, namely social teachers like peers, family and coaches who shape our identity. I asked the class, "What do you recall about your ninth grade physical education teacher?"

A host of answers from unmemorable to striking followed. I had my own example. "My ninth grade PE teacher picked me, a 15-year-old struggling to find my way in a new school, to be the captain of her volleyball team. I balked at the idea because I had never done anything like that. But she persisted. She saw leadership potential in me that I didn't know I had. Today we would call her a mentor. Her confidence in me challenged my beliefs about myself and I gravitated more toward leadership roles."

"The opposite can also be true. Negative messages from important people can be absorbed and influence our self-perceptions. So my question for you today as we go through this program is, 'What beliefs do you hold about yourself that come from others – well-meaning or otherwise – that are simply not true and possibly keep you from living life fully?'" I paused, letting them ponder.

> *"What beliefs do you hold about yourself that come from others that are simply not true and possibly keep you from living life fully?"*

"And those beliefs can be part of what we call emotional anchors. My husband is an avid river fisherman and sometimes does so from a boat. When he and his buddy find their fishing hole, the first thing they do is drop anchor. Why?"

"To keep them in that place. Otherwise they'd float out to the ocean." Jesse explained.

"Exactly. And what happens if, when they want to go home, they forget to pull up the anchor?"

"Not much!"

"Right again, Jesse! In fact, they might burn out the engine trying to drag the anchor along the rocky river floor. It's similar with us. When we anchor ourselves in truth and safe communities we are kept from being swept off course. But when we hold onto negative beliefs or bitterness, we're fighting against ourselves." I scanned the faces to gage how people were doing.

"Beth, you look pretty thoughtful. Anything you'd like to share?" I asked.

"I've been here in this program for all of two days and I've thought more about my life than I have in the last 40 years! It kind of makes my brain hurt." Beth's comments were met with affirming smiles.

"Yes, it is hard work getting to know ourselves. You may find as you go through these next few weeks that you are more tired at the end of each day than if you'd done physical labor for six hours. Emotional work and brain work are taxing."

Beth asked, "Back to what you were talking about with our personalities. Are you saying that we keep changing throughout our lives? Like today I'm not who I was when I was ten and I won't be this person the day I die?"

"That's a great question and the answer is yes, and no. We've just talked about some aspects of our personality that fluctuate or change over our lifetime. We acquire new skills, experience different age-stages, encounter influential people, walk through grief – and so much more that affects our identity.

There are, however, certain aspects of us that are hard-wired from birth and that bedrock of our personality goes with us across our lifespan. Let's look at that now."

I introduced the Personal Style Indicator, a tool we used to increase self and other-awareness and provide a foundation for the rest of the program.

# You've Got Style

Each person completed the Personal Style Indicator and looked at their scores in the four categories – Behavioral (B), Cognitive (C), Interpersonal (I) and Affective (A). While everyone had points in all categories, the index suggests that scores over 40 in any one category is part of one's primary style pattern. People eagerly awaited explanation of the numbers and letters.

"Let's begin with the Behavioral style. How many of you have a score of 40 or higher here?" I inquired. Only one hand went up and the rest looked surprised.

"It's common that there aren't many Behaviorals here because they typically think they can find work on their own. Behaviorals are task-oriented and their approach to life is characterized by action. They are leaders, risk takers, do-ers, and act quickly to get the outcomes they desire. They make projects happen! Much gets done in life because of these people."

"Oh wow, you just described my last boss!" Elise exclaimed. "He was such a jerk. He'd just walk into the meeting, announce the changes he'd put in motion and leave without any time for discussion or questions. Sometimes he literally wouldn't even stay long enough to sit down. Then we'd all be left with almost no information and be expected to make it work."

"Elise, you've touched on one of the key reasons I believe in the value of understanding someone's personal style. You just said your boss was a jerk, right?"

"Yeah. He was a jerk. And we called him a lot worse than that!"

"I think I don't want to know what else you called him! But here's something to think about. Is it possible that his approach to work was a style issue and not a 'jerk' issue?"

Elise stared at me, considering the question. "I'm not sure. I'd have to think about that."

"Your boss sounds great. Are we done yet?" asked Veronica, our lone Behavioral. Others in the room laughed uncomfortably.

"You're not joking, are you?" I knew from years of working with Behaviorals that talk bored them and details felt tedious and confining.

"No. Just give me the bottom line and let me go."

"Ah, yes, the bottom line. 'Give me my assignment. Set me free. Don't look over my shoulder. You do your part.' This is the Behavioral approach to work."

Veronica nodded approval but gave no more words.

"And right before our eyes we're seeing a Behavioral approach and because they prefer to do, not talk, they can bulldoze ahead without enough consultation or information. And since you will work with Behaviorals, here's an example of how to communicate effectively with one."

I recalled a previous boss who had a very high Behavioral style and how, when I first began working for him, I'd enter his office and begin chatting casually about family and weather. "Seeing his face was like watching a fog roll in. The more I made 'small talk', the thicker the mist. He disappeared on me. So, I learned to walk up to his desk and with a glint in my eye, smack my hand down saying, 'Mr. Smith, we have a problem.' Immediately I had his attention and his eyes danced with delight, seeming to ask 'A problem? What problem? I love problems!' Then I'd briefly describe the situation, give my proposed solution and ask him what he'd like me to do. Nine times out of ten he'd say, 'Great. Do it.'"

The key point was in the brevity of the discussion and demonstrating my efficiency, forethought and desire to get results – all things Behaviorals highly value. In other words, I spoke his language. Now it was time to turn our attention to the second task-oriented style, the Cognitives.

"Cognitives are also task-focused but their attention is to the detail. They excel when they can work independently in an unrushed, uncluttered space. Cognitives have a natural hard-wiring for organizing and creating systems. If I took you to our front reception area to meet Deanna, you would see evidence of this Cognitive's brilliant work. Behind each cabinet door are a series of shelves, labeled for each day of this program. Every handout is filed and on the door is a list of extra forms that come into the classroom each morning. A substitute worker could function effectively if they were explained the cupboard system. That's what

Cognitives do – take in information, analyze it and create order from chaos."

"And analyze it, and analyze it and analyze it," added Elise, one who scored high in the Cognitive category.

"Yes, I call it analysis paralysis, and it explains why Cognitives find it hard to make decisions. A good decision is a well-researched decision, right?" All five Cognitives agreed.

"But you may ask when is enough information enough? The Internet is the Cognitive's blessed curse because you could research yourself into oblivion. And, what if you make the *wrong* decision?" I smiled.

Carl raised his hand and asked, "What do you mean by that? Wouldn't Cognitives feel confident in deciding because they are so thorough in their research and thinking things through?"

"Absolutely not!" exclaimed Elise. "The very facts I love overwhelm me and I feel swamped by them. More often than not, I avoid choosing until the deadline or some outside force insists on it. Living in my head is exhausting!"

"You've just given a great description of challenges for Cognitives, Elise. They have a tendency toward control in order to avoid surprises – and because they think their way is the 'right' way to do things."

The lone Behavioral spoke up, "Which of course isn't the case. We all know that the Behavioral's way is the only way!"

"Spoken like a true Behavioral," I added as people laughed. "We're laughing, but really, you're serious, aren't you, Veronica?"

"Of course," she confirmed. An uneasy chuckle punctuated the exchange.

"So, back to the Cognitive. If you want to communicate effectively with Cognitives, give them lots of information and also allow time for them to process it and then discuss the details."

Veronica rolled her eyes, "That drives me crazy! Detail me to death."

Elise's eye widened, "You are just like my old boss. I totally could hear him saying that. I would ask for more information and he would get choked and say something rude like, 'Just figure it out and do it'. How was I supposed to figure it out with no facts?"

"And, once again, we have a living example of style at work. There may be times where one style is more suited to a job or situation, but neither is wrong. They are simply different approaches to work. Where this material becomes incredibly practical is when I can look at another person's approach and interpret it as different, not bad. Here's an example from my kids."

> *"Where this material becomes incredibly practical is when I can look at another person's approach and interpret it as different, not bad."*

"Our middle and youngest sons, nine and seven, were playing quietly in their bedroom. All of a sudden the more Cognitive child, Clark, came storming into the living room and launched into an animated rant detailing how his brother ruined their game, wasn't playing by the rules and messed things up. And just as quickly as the tirade began, it stopped. He looked over at me and said, 'Wait a minute. Mom, is this a style issue?' to which I replied, 'Sounds like it could be.'

'So he's not doing that stuff on purpose just to bug me?'

'Maybe not. Maybe he's just different from you.' I responded. Clark stood quietly for a moment, pondering the possibility and then headed back down the hall and re-engaged in play."

"Wow, he was nine and had personalities figured out?" asked Carl.

"'Figured out' might be a bit big but my point is that even children, when taught to interpret someone's behavior as different, not as intentionally irritating, have better life skills."

Elise noted with a grin, "So, I've been thinking, as a good Cognitive does, and I think it's time for a coffee break."

"I agree. And when we come back, we'll talk about the two people-oriented styles, Interpersonals and Affectives."

The group returned to the classroom with unusual levels of chatter and interaction. "Sounds like you've had stimulating coffee talk. Let's carry on with the remaining two categories. First, we have the Interpersonal style."

I explained how the Interpersonal is naturally drawn to the needs of people over tasks. They thrive when given opportunities to love others and are known for giving compassionate care to people in practical ways. They enjoy one-to-one or small group connections where deeper emotional sharing happens. Interpersonals are loyal, hard-working employees who prefer behind-the-scenes positions and not the center of attention. They are great listeners and peacemakers.

"Peacemakers?" asked Veronica.

"As in, they don't like conflict. They like harmonious relationships."

Carl nodded in agreement, "Oh yes, I hate conflict of any kind. I find it hard to be in the room even when my kids are arguing over a toy. It makes me feel awful."

"And that becomes one of the greatest challenges for Interpersonals – the need to see conflict as natural and possible to navigate through, not just avoid."

"No, I'd rather sweep it under the carpet," Carl volunteered, fidgeting in his chair and adjusting his papers.

"The difficulty becomes the lumpy carpet which we're bound to trip over."

"Not if you spend a life time learning to sneak around the lumps," Carl offered.

"So then I guess my question is what does that kind of maneuvering cost you?"

"I'm just incredibly flexible!"

"Like the old cartoon guys, Gumby and Pokey, I'm guessing!"

"Yes, exactly." Carl smiled.

"It's true. Interpersonals have a capacity to flex to the needs of others and that can be a desirable quality in a support role. Unfortunately the down side is that Interpersonals may do so at the cost of their own needs going unmet. They give and give and give and then one day this kind-natured, helping person quits or blows up or breaks down and friends and co-workers are baffled because the Interpersonal hadn't let on there was an ongoing problem."

"So in order to be healthy it's important for Interpersonals to remember to take care of themselves first – like the instruction you get on an airplane – 'Put on your own oxygen mask before helping anyone else.' And it's helpful if Interpersonals keep in mind that while they think they can read people's minds, they really can't!"

"Are you sure about that?" asked Carl in all seriousness. "I can walk into a room, scan it and know how people are doing."

"Using that emotional radar, hey? Okay, what emotion does *this* look convey to you about me?" I put on a pensive face, eye brows lowered, eyes focused intently at the floor.

"You are really stressed and worried." Carl assessed.

"In some people that could definitely be the case. But if I have a high Cognitive score it could be that I'm thinking and analyzing a situation. And if that's the case I may be having a great time – in my head!" The group laughed.

Veronica added, "And if that was my face it would mean 'I'm working – which is fun for me – so leave me alone!'"

"So the point is we need to check our assumptions. Interpersonals get into trouble in situations like this: I phone an Interpersonal friend who I haven't talked to in a while. She mentions she's moved and I convey surprise that she didn't ask me to help. She replies, 'Oh I assumed you're really busy and wouldn't have been able to help so I didn't ask.'"

"I hate it when people do that," blurted out Veronica. "I'm a big girl. Let me decide for myself."

"And that's precisely the point. If, as an Interpersonal, I don't want to ask someone else for help, that's fine. But I must decide that from *my* needs, not because I think I know what *you* need or want."

Carl conceded, "Yeah, I have gotten into a few sticky situations where I thought I was helping but the friend was ticked. I couldn't understand why but what you've said makes sense of it."

"We also know that Interpersonals will respond best if they feel included, connected and treated with kindness. They are not weak people, nor do they want you to sugar-coat the truth. They want honest interaction, just not with great intensity. Gentleness matters. And if you really want to relate well with Interpersonals then show care and concern for people they love." I paused in case there were questions. None. Not surprising. Interpersonals often preferred to stick around after class to connect privately.

"Are we ready to meet the Affectives?" I shifted gears.

"Finally!" grinned the person with the highest Affective score in the room.

"It's hard work waiting to become the center of attention, isn't it Affectives?" The Cognitive and Interpersonals looked confused as the three Affectives responded. "Absolutely! I thought you'd never get to us!"

"The stage is yours now! Actually, the world is the stage for the Affective."

"Yeah!" cheered Anna, while Carl and Elise looked on, perplexed.

"Let me introduce you to the second people-loving style, the Affectives. This group loves to acquaint and connect with diverse people. They are born to network and thrive on opportunities to creatively influence others. Affectives are idea people who love to talk and tell animated stories. They are drawn to jobs like teaching, sales, marketing, motivational speaking – anything involving lots of people, fun, attention and variety."

"You've totally described me!" shouted Anna. "If I had my dream job, I'd travel around the world meeting and training people on how to set up small, self-sustaining businesses. I would get investors to buy into the model and give people in impoverished places interest free loans to cover their start-up costs. It would be the best."

Elise leaned forward, interest peaked by the plan. "What criteria would you use to determine who received the funding and how would you manage the loan payback?"

"Oh, I'd figure that out later. The point is…" Anna was interrupted by a distressed looking Elise.

*"Do you see where there is room for conflict if we don't understand one another's differences? Or the prospect of great collaboration if we do?"*

"I think it is a major point that you are overlooking. You won't be able to sell investors on the idea if you don't have documentation to support the integrity of their investment." Elise looked serious.

Anna replied, un-phased, "I'm not worried about that. Hey, I could hire you to take care of that."

I jumped in just before Elise could launch another rebuttal. "And here again style reveals itself. Let's step back and talk about what just happened. Anna has a wonderful idea that she's enthusiastic about. She sees the big picture, the potential to change lives and the adventure of travel. What she doesn't see are the finer points because Affectives are not drawn to detail."

"Clearly," mumbled Elise.

"And Cognitive Elise gave immediate attention to the practical aspects of making the plan work. Do you see where there is room for conflict if we don't understand one another's differences? Or the prospect of great collaboration if we do? We need Affectives' outside-the-box ideas and then they need to be set free to do other creative endeavors. Affectives are typically not great implementers or maintainers. They get bored with routine."

"Affectives have such a strong orientation to people that they struggle with task and time management. People distract them – as do creative projects – making focus a challenge. In fact, any shiny thing in the corner can lure them away."

The Affectives agreed that the world is full of shiny things. Anna added, "And what you said about time management... oh my goodness, have I ever been on time for anything in my whole life? I was even overdue as a baby!"

"Wear a watch," Veronica suggested impatiently.

I jumped in. "Yes, brilliant insight, if you think to put one on! In fact when I survey Affectives to see who is wearing a watch, occasionally one will be. The amusing thing is that often the watch isn't working or, in one case, was worn upside down!"

Elise looked shocked. "You've got to be kidding me? Why wear a broken watch?"

Without coordination Anna and Sam – another Affective – shouted, "Because it's a fashion accessory; because it's cute!"

"Good grief," remarked Elise, to which Veronica added, "Unbelievable."

Anna responded buoyantly, "Nope, like I said before, Shelaine has just described my whole life. Give me ideas and fun, leave the details out and expect me to be late to everything. Yup, that's me in a nutshell!"

We spent the next few minutes summarizing each style and how to recognize them in others.

"Our best method, apart from carrying around a pocket full of Personal Style Indicators, is to become students of the people around us. For example, a couple years back we had reason to mix up the seating arrangement part way through the program. The morning after we did so it was fascinating to watch people respond by style. A Cognitive arrived first and headed for her spot. She stopped abruptly, looked at the name tag placement and turned to me asking, "Why are the name tags changed? What happened? Is this a mistake or did you do this on purpose?"

"An Interpersonal walked in next and immediately noted the difference. She came over to my desk and quietly said, 'I will sit where my name tag is but I was just getting to know Melissa. Will I get to sit by her again later? She's having a really hard time.'"

I proceeded with the story. "An Affective entered the room, oblivious to the name cards, but saw people in different seats. 'Hey, this is great,' she bubbled, 'new neighbors. Where do I sit?' The Cognitive pointed her to her name tag. With that the Behavioral arrived. He scanned the room, walked over to his name plate and grabbed it off the table. 'This isn't where I sit' and promptly went to his old spot."

"Wow, I guess style shows up even in seating arrangements," observed Carl.

"Yes, understanding Personal Style has revolutionized my world. It has changed my marriage, my parenting, and my work. Let me wrap up today with one last story from my family.

Our middle son, about twelve at the time, entered the kitchen with an inquisitive expression. He stood quietly beside me as I washed dishes. 'Mom, I've been in my room thinking. I was wondering, if you could add an extra body part, what would you add?'

> *"Mom, I've been in my room thinking. If you could add an extra body part, what would you add?"*

Caught completely unprepared for such a question, I bought some time by responding with, 'That's a fascinating question, Clark. What body part would you add?'

He paused and took on the intensity of one solving matters of deep importance and considered the question as if new to himself. 'Well,' he ventured after several seconds, 'I would add an extra ear. But it would be a special ear. It would be on top of my head and would allow me to hear what other people are thinking and feeling.' Interesting, I thought. Clark is a Cognitive Interpersonal – a thinker-feeler.

At that moment our oldest son, a Behavioral, entered. Still stalling and searching for my own response I asked, 'Hey Taylor. Your brother has a great question for you. If you could add an extra body part, what would you add?'

'What kind of stupid question is that?' he replied without hesitation.

'Oh come on,' I cajoled, 'lighten up and answer the question.'

'Fine. I'd add a tail like a monkey so I could go places faster and get more done in a day.'

Hearing the party in the kitchen our youngest and Affective son Eric came bounding in. 'What are you guys doing?'

'Hey Eric, Clark has a question for you,' I said, thankful for more time to think while Clark reiterated the inquiry to his brother.

'Eric, if you could add an extra body part, what would you add?'

Without taking a breath Eric replied, 'Oh, that's easy. I'd add an extra head. That way I'd never be alone and I'd always have someone to talk to.'"

"That's hilarious!" commented Anna. "Shelaine, you never said what body part you'd add."

I smiled coyly. "And look at the time. We're all done for today. See you tomorrow!"

## WHY ISN'T SHOWING UP ENOUGH?

# "Hello-oo!"

We were several days into our month-long course. Cheri, one of our twelve participants, sat at the back of the classroom on the short end of the horseshoe arrangement of tables. Granted, she was almost as far as she could be from the door, but our adherence to fire code did ensure she had a clear path of exit from the classroom. This is important to note.

I sat on my stool at the front in the center by the PowerPoint projector fully engaged in sharing a story. A *bleep* from the back caught my attention and slowed my thinking. I carried on as Cheri reached down into her orange purse – the one I'm sure would not meet carry-on luggage size restrictions – and began digging with both hands for the noise-maker.

Fully capturing the class' attention now, I paused my story as she victoriously pulled out her phone, swiped, and announced, "Hello-oo!" I wanted to be gracious because we all forget to turn off our phones periodically so I made eye contact and extended my left hand toward her. I gently motioned for her to move down the side of the room and exit into the adjacent hallway. She smiled and kept talking. Believing she hadn't fully grasped my sign language, I repeated the gesture and, once again, she beamed and carried on with her conversation.

Baffled and slightly irritated now, I tried words. "Cheri, please take your call out in the hallway," to which she promptly replied with all sincerity, "Oh no, it's okay. You aren't bothering me." Several class members' eyebrows raised.

The image we project to the world wherever we go is an often overlooked component in the job transition process. Cheri had me and eleven others looking on and forming opinions about her suitability as a worker as she chatted away. In that short incident, Cheri revealed several values and raised red flags about her awareness of workplace codes. When her conversation ended I set aside the current topic and began a discussion about job maintenance.

*Several participants had never given consideration to what their at-work behavior looked like to a boss.*

"Before we carry on, Cheri, I'm wondering if we could talk about what just happened there," to which she answered buoyantly, "Sure, it was my friend asking if I could have coffee after class!"

"That's not exactly what I mean. If this were a work situation how would you have handled that phone call?"

"Just like I did now. Is that a problem? Wouldn't you guys do the same thing?" she asked, looking around to her classmates for input.

Tom volunteered, "My previous employer had a 'no personal calls' policy so that would have been a big problem at my last job."

Lucy added, "We were told that personal calls or texting were grounds for discipline because we worked with so much confidential information. The organization had to protect its clients so we had to turn off our personal phones."

"Seriously?" asked Cheri. "You could get into trouble for using your cell phone at work? Why?"

"Let's think about it from the employer's perspective. What does your personal call mean for them?" I inquired.

Tom began, "Well, they are paying me to do a job and if I'm doing personal stuff on company time, it's like I'm stealing from them."

"Stealing!" gasped Cheri. "I wasn't trying to steal anything from anybody!"

The conversation continued as we explored a workplace reality through the eyes of employers and supervisors. Several participants had never given consideration to what their at-work behavior looked like to a boss. I posed the question, "If you were in charge, what would give you confidence in your employee? What would you like to see in someone you are supervising?"

Tom offered, "I would definitely notice if someone was on time or not. That's another place people steal from the company – arriving late, leaving early, taking extra-long breaks."

Cheri grimaced at the mention of theft again and changed the subject. "I want to be the boss of happy people. I hate working with sour-faced people who act like coming to work is torture. I like my job and want to be around people who like theirs."

Cheri had touched on a core concept for career success. Many times when I've worked with companies doing hiring interviews we have had preliminary discussions about what they want in an employee. They almost always mention attitude right away. In fact, many companies have a philosophy of "hire for attitude, train for skill." You can teach people new skills but attitude affects everything – even how willing someone is to learn a new skill.

*You can teach people new skills, but attitude affects everything – even how willing someone is to learn a new skill.*

In addition a negative attitude is behind several reasons people are let go from their positions. Insubordination (refusing to follow orders or submit to authority), inappropriate use of company property, misconduct (immoral, unethical or unprofessional behavior), drug or alcohol use or possession at work, and taking too much time off are a few examples of attitude-rooted issues resulting in dismissal. A person's mind-set and point-of-view also influence their ability to navigate workplace relationships.

We returned to the question, "What makes a good employee?"and generated a list: playing nicely with others or being easy to get along with; giving their best effort; celebrating the successes of others; having a 'can do' attitude, not an Eeyore approach; being confident and willing to ask questions or request help; managing their time and schedule effectively; taking initiative within reasonable boundaries; handling conflict appropriately and in a timely manner; having a sense of humor and ability to laugh at themselves, not others; taking good ideas or processes and making them better.

I concluded the brainstorming with this, "Underlying many characteristics we've identified is an attitude that I would summarize this way. An employee who stands out is one who thinks of what they can do for the company, not just what the company can do for them. If we use that as a guiding principle we are more likely to make choices that will set us apart and, in the big picture, serve us well too."

# End Well

"I was too busy filling orders and maintaining inventory to be researching computers. Besides, I was keeping up, records were accurate and I knew where to find everything. I didn't need a computer!" The cords in Gerry's neck bulged and her volume increased. She wasn't finished yet.

"My boss kept bugging me about looking into computers for almost a year. That would have been a waste of my time. I had more important things to do – like my job!" Gerry scoffed and took a breath. "And then, one day out of the blue, my boss shows up with this young guy and introduces him as the new techy. *Efficiencies*, my boss called it, as if I didn't do efficient work. Before I knew it, I was fired and that 'child' had my job. There's no respect for seniority or loyalty anymore. I worked for that company for 31 years and just like that, for no good reason, I'm gone."

Gerry maintained this story throughout our three-week course and became visibly agitated when asked anything about her previous work experience. She experienced difficulty isolating skills she possessed and often ranted about the injustice of being replaced. I met with Gerry individually at the end of the class sessions. After she spewed more about her unfair treatment, I asked Gerry this question.

"If your previous employer came to see me and I asked him to describe his side of your dismissal story, what do you think he would say?"

"He'd say he was a jerk and never should have fired such a loyal worker." Gerry smirked sheepishly. "Well, maybe not exactly that."

> *"If your previous employer came to see me and I asked him to describe his side of your dismissal story, what do you think he would say?"*

I persisted. "How about you start his story from when he requested that you research an inventory control program. What did he say to you?"

"Well, he approached me at the end of a coffee break and asked when I could sit down and talk with him about the computer thing. I told him I was too busy and it would have to be the next week."

"And, did you talk the next week?" I inquired.

"No, I guess we never did sit down and talk about it. I had so much work to do and he was asking me to do more. And, he was asking me to do stuff I knew nothing about." Gerry's hands tightened into fists.

I returned to my original question. "So how would your boss tell me about that experience with you?"

"Oh, he'd likely say I started avoiding him, that I'd brush him off whenever he brought up the topic…I guess he would say that I never did what he asked me to do...but I was very busy!" Gerry met my eyes with an insistent glare.

"Okay," I added, "so your boss asked you to do something several times over a long period of time and you didn't do it. Then what happened, from your employer's perspective?"

Gerry's neck and cheeks reddened. "I don't know. I guess he got frustrated and decided he couldn't wait any longer. So, he hired that young buck to do the computer work and before you know it, I'm out on the street!"

"So how did that exchange go? Can you tell me as if it is your boss giving me the story?"

"Well, he brought the kid – Karl was his name – into the office and introduced me. He said that Karl would be following me around to learn how I did my job and then he would take all my paper systems and turn them into something on the computer. And then, before I knew it, I was fired."

The story felt like it had gaps so I asked a few more questions. "Did anything else happen between the introduction and you being let go?"

Gerry's head dropped and she shifted in her chair. "I may have said something."

"Gerry, what would your employer tell me you said?"

Gerry sighed deeply, stared into the floor and began hesitantly. "He would tell you that I got angry – so angry that I picked up a book from my desk and threw it across the room. Then he would probably tell you that I stood and screamed at him – I don't even remember everything I said but it was about being loyal and not being appreciated and being asked to do too much and then…" her voice trailed off.

"And then?" I asked gently.

"And then I used words I've never used before in my life. It's like I lost control. I called him horrible names and said awful things that weren't even true. He really had been very good to me over the years but I couldn't take the pressure and I stood there and screamed at him…for a long time…in front of this kid."

Tears ran down Gerry's cheeks as she spoke softly. "So, I suppose if my boss were telling you this story he would say that he tried to get me to change to a new system and I wouldn't do it. He hired someone trained in what I wasn't, to do what I wouldn't. He would likely say I was stubborn and set in my ways. And, he would likely tell you that I had a break down and yelled and swore at him and that he doesn't tolerate that from any employee, even one that's been there as long as me." She took a long breath and looked up at me.

*"What do I do now? It was all my fault I lost the job and now here I am, too old and too scared to learn new things."*

"What do I do now? It was all my fault I lost the job and now here I am, too old and too scared to learn new things."

"Let's start with the ending of your job, first. We know that your time with that company is over so that can't be changed. But if you could have ended it differently, what would that look like?"

"Well, it sure wouldn't involve me swearing at my boss. I guess I wish I had told him early on that I didn't know how to find out about computers. I was embarrassed that I didn't know. Maybe if I had admitted that, we could have figured something out a year ago."

"So Gerry, speaking up sooner and talking to your boss is something you wish you had done differently. What would it take for you to feel like you ended well…or at least better than it is right now?"

Gerry broke eye contact again, "I don't know. I feel so ashamed of how I acted. I can't undo that. So I'm not sure what to say."

"Think of it this way. If you were to meet him in a store, what needs to happen so you can look him in the eye as you walk by?" I proposed.

Gerry sat quietly and then offered, "I know I need to apologize." She grabbed her stomach, "Oh, even saying that makes me feel sick. I don't think I'm that brave."

"Well, if meeting him in person feels too big, would you consider writing him a letter?" My question was answered initially by Gerry's heaving sigh and shaking head. I waited and watched her demeanor soften.

"Maybe I could do that," Gerry volunteered. "I want to do something. I hate living like this. I could try to write a letter."

She did write the apology letter and mailed it. While I never read it, I noted visible change in Gerry's demeanor and story at our three-month follow-up appointment.

Many of our clients apologized for their part in the loss of a job and returned to tell me of the closure they experienced. They spoke of holding their heads up again and not feeling such shame. Not all people experienced open arms of reconciliation with previous employers, but many spoke of a freedom that came in knowing they had done everything within their power to make things right. What happens in one situation – and how we process it – becomes stitched into the fabric of who we are and how we show up in the rest of life. It's important to end well.

# Wish List

Evelyn sat at the end of the table closest to the door. She requested this spot for quick escape just in case the classroom didn't have enough air. Her most recent work experience damaged her belief in the human race and she made it clear upon registration that attending the class was a horrible idea. She agreed to take one day at a time with the understanding that she could bail if needed. She never did.

In fact by the end of the program Evelyn refused to leave. She playfully announced at the celebration lunch that she would be back for the first day of the next class and for each one ever after. She dubbed herself the poster child of the course.

Evelyn embodied the ideal in our program – a person who had found a safe place to reflect on and grieve past work experiences, gathered support during a lonely and confusing time, and began exploring realistic next steps. She came to us deflated, beaten down and convinced that her life would remain in ruins. In the end she soared. The difference was impossible to miss.

But then the class finished and her motivation for getting out of bed dried up. She now had to initiate setting up meeting times with friends from class. Together she and alumni began dropping off resumes with potential employers, but with no success. The rejections piled up and Evelyn's confidence plummeted. She sat in my office at her one-month follow-up appointment discouraged and terrified as her bank account bottomed out and her Employment Insurance neared its end.

"I don't understand," Evelyn shook her head as she began to speak. "I left here higher than a kite. I felt so pumped up I thought I could take on the world. I'm beginning to wonder if I'll ever find a job. I really don't have much to offer."

"Evelyn, it's pretty common to feel a letdown after such an intensely positive experience, which is what I've heard you say this was for you."

Evelyn broke her stare at the floor and responded immediately, "Oh, these three weeks changed my life…it maybe even saved my life. I was sure I would never work again and you know, after the way my last boss treated me, I wasn't sure I ever wanted to work again!"

Picking up on her recollection of the positive time I asked, "Can you remind me of the things you discovered about yourself here?"

Evelyn talked about how she now viewed her ability to quickly learn a task and then do it accurately and efficiently as a desirable feature to an employer. "I just did it. I never knew it was something special or different from other workers."

"And what else changed while you were here?" I asked.

"I realized that I want to work with my hands alongside the right number of people. I need tasks and some people in the work I do. I'm not asking for too much, am I?"

"No, I don't think so. There are lots of jobs that have a mix of people and tasks. It's a matter of you finding one that fits you. Anything else come to mind from your time here?"

"It's funny. I never did well in school so I always thought I was stupid. I wouldn't say I'm really smart but you guys helped me see that I can learn. And what's even funnier to me, I realized that I like math." We laughed together as I asked, "How did we help you figure out that?"

"When we did those skills assessments I kept picking things that needed math. I really do like that but I could never do accounting or something so I can't see how that would help me in a job."

"Well, let's think for a minute about work that uses math in a practical way but isn't only about math." Evelyn's puzzled expression prompted me to explain. "Take construction, for example, it's full of measuring things using math in order to do the task."

"I see what you're saying, but I'm really not strong enough to swing a hammer all day!" Some of the sparkle we'd seen develop in Evelyn returned to her eyes. "And, I don't own a tool belt!"

"Fair enough. Would you be okay with spending a few minutes here looking at some postings online? I find that sometimes it's helpful to have a second set of eyes that might see something you'd pass over."

"Sure, why not? You're the expert!" she teased.

"I don't know about that but this is my job so I get to practice this all the time. Makes a difference – I hope."

I navigated to my favorite job search listings and read a few out to her that seemed reasonable. We printed off four possibilities before I came to a Quality Control Technician – food processing (Lab Technician) position. She sat forward in her chair as I read out the job title.

"Now that sounds like a cool position. What qualifications do they want?" As quickly as her interest soared she deflated when I reviewed the desired skills and experience, including a science background.

"That's what I face all the time. I get excited about something and then I read what they want and I don't have it. What am I going to do?" she bemoaned.

"Apply, of course." I replied.

"I thought you were the expert here," Evelyn chided. "Or is your hearing bad? I just said I don't have any of those qualifications!"

I challenged her, "Well, that's not entirely true. You have the 'ability to work efficiently in a dynamic and fast paced environment' and I know you are 'detail and result oriented' and you possess 'good organizational skills', right? And they want someone who has 'good interpersonal and teamwork ability', 'problem solving and trouble-shooting abilities' and is 'self-motivated'. Sounds like you to me!"

She conceded but quickly offered her protest, "Yes, but you happen to be ignoring all the *real* qualifications like 'understanding of common analytical instrumentation' or 'background in science'.

"The *real* ones? Evelyn, let me ask you something. Do you think it's easier to teach someone to run a piece of equipment or to be an effective team player?"

Evelyn thought for a moment and answered "the equipment" so I pressed on. "I agree and so do many employers. When a company needs to hire, they put together their wish list and call it a job ad. Why not put everything you hope an ideal candidate will have out there and then see who applies? That said I've heard many employers use the phrase, 'hire for character, train for skill.'"

Evelyn beamed, "Well, I'm certainly enough of a character!"

> *"I've heard many employers use the phrase, 'hire for character, train for skill.'"*

"Yes, you are! So, what do you think?"

"What do I have to lose in applying, right?" she asked.

I nodded in agreement and we put together a new cover letter, highlighting her related experience and transferable skills. She left the office, committed to submitting applications and resumes to anything that interested her. After all, what did she have to lose?

About three weeks later our office administrator let me know that Evelyn had a full time job. She had called to say thank you and to let us know that she now worked as a Quality Control Technician in a food processing plant. That was the last we heard from her until I bumped into Evelyn in a produce store two-and-a-half years later. She volunteered more of her story in her delightful, animated manner.

"I've been working all this time in the lab of that company you suggested I apply to! I thought you were nuts but I figured I might as well try. I couldn't believe it when I got called in for the interview. The woman who met with me really liked me and told me that they normally didn't hire someone to work in the lab with no science background." She paused and smiled sheepishly. "I know, I know. I guess they really do make exceptions when they like you! Oh, and they do like me! In fact, they regularly tell me what a great job I'm doing and how happy they are to have me. Can you believe it?"

"Well, actually I can! You have so much to offer. They are fortunate to have you."

Standing in the produce aisle, for all to hear, she added, "When I came to your program, I was a mess. You know, I actually believe that it was a good thing I got fired from that other job because this one is way better!" Evelyn went on to describe her financial stability, the new place she moved into and her general love of life.

Evelyn reminded me of how often people will opt out of the running for a job because they don't meet all the posted criteria. Few people can satisfy an employer's every wish but those who have courage to apply anyway may just sell the interviewer with their character, attitude and trainability. Evelyn did.

**WHO CARES?**

## Betty's Story

"Shelaine. Come. Here. Now!"

The scream interrupted my post-teaching fog as I contemplated a cup of tea. I had been watching the milk swirl into the brown liquid and savoring every sip, a reward as I reviewed the day. Agreeable group, no huge attitudes, they like each other and all ten are working well together. They were a yellow group, using the rainbow spectrum of informal class ratings. Not beige, but not quite fuchsia either. Nothing out of the ordinary, I was beginning to conclude. The shrill command from our receptionist down the hall tidying up, however, was far from the norm. I set down my tea and jogged to the classroom. At the sight of me, Amy proclaimed, "There is Poop. On. The. Chair!!!" She punctuated 'poop' most strongly and 'chair' a close second.

"What?" I asked, my sensibilities offended and confused. I just spent the day in this room. Wouldn't I have known if someone had relieved themselves during a discussion on job search? How did I not smell it? I recalled the faces around the tables, trying to draw up expressions of discomfort. Nothing. How could I have missed a mid-day, in-class, on-chair bowel movement?

"There is Poooop…" Amy began again.

"Right, I get it. I heard you the first time. I'm just shocked. I've never had *this* happen before." I paused, scrambling to find an appropriate response to news of fecal matter on fabric seat. I stumbled, "Do you know whose chair it is?"

> *"I've never had this happen before."*

"Oh course," she retorted, glaring at the name tag by the chair. I considered Amy's sharp reaction and the unpleasant task ahead of her and let the comment go. The woozy churn in my stomach tightened as I pictured her scrubbing the mess, eased only as I secretly gave thanks for my job. My nausea returned when Amy broke the silence, "So, when will you talk with Betty?"

Oh. My. Yes, that would be my job. I suddenly felt the need to sit down – in a clean chair. People came to us in work, career and life transitions and our job was to help prepare them for not only getting a job but for keeping it as well. I envisioned our client soiling a chair in an interview, standing up to leave – oh, stop it! I hardly reined in that scene and another followed. There she was, in her workplace, leaving feces behind as she walked away from her desk. Good grief. I stared through Betty's name plate sickened over the distress she could face and uneasy as to how I would handle this.

"Okay, okay, I'll talk to her," I blurted anxiously. Amy turned, "I know. That's your job."

Typically our staff worked cooperatively, covering off one another and helping out when workloads weighed heavily. We also had job descriptions like classroom instructor, resume writer or receptionist. To this point, however, no one had been specifically assigned bodily fluids advisor. I had in the past entered into several uncomfortable conversations with people about things like the need to shower – to which one client replied, "Oh, I do, every month." I had hoped his interviews corresponded with his routine.

Charged with the task of explaining how employment success was connected to bad breath or wild smiles, multiple clients and I had chatted privately about personal survival, resilience and quirky circumstances. Take Joe. Missing more teeth than he possessed, Joe gave account for each gap. The front left one got knocked out in a bar fight when he was nineteen. Living on the street for years meant he rarely owned a toothbrush and mouthwash was only a cheap tide-me-over to the next real drink. Some mornings, Joe explained, he woke up and found a chiclet or two lying beside him from gums weakened due to excessive alcohol and smoking. Beyond me referring him to a lengthy waitlist for free dental care, all I could offer was empathy.

I also recalled approaching a man about the clothing he planned to wear to his interview noting that while they looked clean enough the wrinkles screamed he had slept in them. Scared silly at the prospect of even a mock interview he explained that he had gotten dressed the night before to lessen his morning routine. We brainstormed other time-saving measures.

# CHANGING COURSE

One of my fellow instructors had a client suddenly turn her back to the class and vomit in the garbage can. Another participant peed on the leather couch in our boss' office during a practice interview. While I did have an exchange with the client about the urine issue, I must confess, I never mentioned it to my boss.

So, it's not as if I felt unpracticed discussing sensitive issues with clients. Somehow this one just felt harder. As I lay in bed that night I reviewed my options with Betty. I could ignore the issue with hopes that it wouldn't happen again – at least while she's in our class. Selfish, I concluded. I could call in sick. Cowardly. I could even hand in my resignation. Way too melodramatic. Or I could simply talk to her. But how?

What's the best way to begin? I questioned the ceiling at 2 a.m. "Betty, how are you feeling these days, intestinally speaking?" No, a more direct approach would be better. "Betty, there was poop on your chair." Oh, that's so cold. I tried other lines: "When Amy was cleaning up the other day, she noticed something on your chair." Or "We simply can't have people pooping in class." Oh help! Three a.m. ticked by providing fewer and fewer brilliant insights.

Sometime after four the question came, *What makes talking to Betty so frightening for me?* I'm not easily shocked or intimidated by bizarre client comments anymore, so it can't be that. Anger doesn't throw me like it once did. And raising three boys provided ample discussions about body waste and similarly gross subjects, so I doubted it was poop-o-phobia.

And then it dawned on me. Humiliation! If I were on the other side of this situation as the one being confronted about my toileting habits, I would be mortified. I'm embarrassed for her and I'm uncomfortable with how this will make her feel. So if the roles were reversed, how would I want to be treated?

Morning came too early. I felt spent, but clear on my direction. As I got dressed and ate breakfast I resolved to speak with Betty that day. It sat well in my spirit and I double-dosed on deodorant.

Selfishly I wanted to have the conversation right away. My path was set and I did not want to anticipate the talk for six teaching hours. But how would it be for her to be pulled into my office and start her day this way? Would she crumble, go home and miss important content and group interaction? Could she stay and sit through the class looking at me? Could I make eye contact with her?

*So if the roles were reversed, how would I want to be treated?*

My debate ended abruptly when my boss approached the office doorway. He wanted one of his clients to sit in on my teaching – yes, today, and proceeded to introduce me. Oh, and could I sit down with his client for a few minutes – yes, right now, and answer a few of his questions about the program. I had my answer. The Betty conversation would have to wait.

On the afternoon coffee break I asked Betty if she would stay for a few minutes at the end of the day. Yes, she could. I directed her into our private office area after class, unsure if I was relieved or disappointed. I began with something like, "Betty, I really don't know how to better talk to you about this than to simply say I am concerned about how you are. We found some feces on your chair yesterday and I'm wondering what that could be about."

Betty's eyes filled with tears as her gaze dropped. We were quiet together.

"I...I...have trouble getting to the bathroom fast enough," she hesitated but began again, voice quivering, eyes avoiding mine. "I have Rheumatoid arthritis and it affects everything. It's so embarrassing." Head drooping, she sobbed quietly.

I handed her a tissue and she carried on, sharing how depression zapped her motivation; she hadn't vacuumed her apartment in over a year; bank account empty; Social Assistance cheques barely covering rent; food banks and soup kitchens feeding her – when she could get there. Wounds, losses, and deficits pressed in as I listened. Her hardships, so immense; my offerings, so meager.

When her story felt told, I asked if I could have Amy look into some resources for her. She nodded as her eyes met mine for the first time since we began. Betty stood up and opened the office door to leave, then turned back. "Thank you for caring enough about me to have this conversation. No one has ever done anything like this for me before."

I savored another cup of tea and considered our conversation. She had thanked me for listening to her story, for extending compassion. My body ached and longed to go home but I lingered with my thoughts. Somewhere deep in that place where knowing is and words are not yet formed my journeying with clients took a greener path.

SHELAINE STROM

# Perils of Instructing

Park the car. Get out and balance on right foot. Secure pack of teaching materials onto back. Reach for crutches and head across the parking lot. Typical day. My new normal. A persistent foot injury required hobbling on two wooden sticks. While I accepted my limitations at home and work, each morning held one activity I dreaded.

This office, on the second floor of an older building, had one twelve-foot wide, life-threatening bank of stairs. I opted for the next worst choice – the service elevator.

I navigated into the back lobby and caught my breath. I don't recall having questioned the term "service elevator" prior to this stage of my life. The metal box on pulley cables required a button be pushed to open the door, a button to close the door, and continuous pressure on another button to tell the elevator to move. Any slip of my finger off that button and the suspended container lurched to an immediate mid-air stop. Thankfully, most days, simply pushing the button again resumed the journey.

Today my finger slipped.

The elevator jerked to a standstill and I pondered the term "service elevator" more deeply. Perhaps the name fit because of prayer services people held hoping to survive the trip to floor two. More likely, I mused as the machine squawked, rattled and jerked, its name derived from the memorial service to be held when police discovered my body three months later. I held my breath, then let it go as the door opened on my floor. Safe again.

Our rectangular classroom walls were dotted with framed inspirational quotations such as, *When you change the way you look at things, the things you look at change* and *There is no I in Team*. I crutched over to the fourth wall before the participants arrived and opened the vertical blinds to let in some west coast overcast.

"Good morning, welcome back," I greeted each one as I tucked my crutches into my ribs and began. "Today we are going to talk about Career Decision Making or in other words, 'What do you want to be when you grow up?'"

"I have to grow up?" jested Jim.

"Good quest…" My words trailed off as the floor shifted and the blinds swayed. I grabbed the crutch handles. Yes, I was upright, but the sensation of tilting didn't stop and neither did the blinds. In an instant, they were swinging left and right, fully a foot back and forth.

What on earth is happening?! It can't be wind. The windows are permanently sealed. Air conditioning doesn't move the floor. "Earthquake!" I blurted, hardly recognizing my voice.

Now you might think because I live on the west coast where we're reminded regularly to expect the "big one" that I would immediately recognize the signs of an earthquake and know exactly how to proceed. You might also expect that as the instructor of the program I would have emergency procedures memorized, rehearsed and practiced with each new class. And you might also believe that all of this would come together in that split second when the ground beneath my one foot and two crutches began to shift. Ha!

*What on earth is happening?!*
*It can't be wind.*
*"Earthquake!"*

I stood there, gaping at eleven stunned faces. *I'm in charge but what am I supposed to do? Is inside safer or should we be running out? Should I direct people under tables? Why didn't I pay closer attention to earthquake safety?*

My mental conversation crashed to a halt as my twelfth client bolted from his chair. Kirk, a man in his mid-thirties, built like a tanker truck and in transition between nursing jobs, headed straight toward me. I began to give instructions, "I think…" but was interrupted by Kirk throwing one arm around my back and the other buckling my knees. In one swift move I went from propped to scooped.

"Stop! Put. Me. Down!" I shouted. I saw bewilderment and shock in the eyes of the classmates and can only imagine what they saw in mine. As Kirk navigated us out the classroom door and to the reception area, I squirmed and pushed at his chest.

"Don't worry. Hold still. I'll get you out of here!"

"Put me down! I have to deal with the class members. I'm in charge here!"

I caught sight of Amy's horror related either to the earthquake or the fact that an instructor was being stolen in broad daylight. She yelled, "Put her down!"

For whatever reason, he did. The building was no longer swaying. I one-foot bounced back into the classroom to find my people silently seated, jaws open, eyes on the door. I hopped back to my spot, secured crutches under my armpits, pushed my hair behind my ears and said, "Now, where were we?"

Today I reflect on that early-career incident and regret not acknowledging the concern Kirk extended to me. I wish I had thanked him for caring and celebrated his quick thinking and action in a crisis instead of succumbing to embarrassment and my own insecurities.

In later years I grew in my ability to be more objective and not take other people's actions personally – like the day my class got up and walked out.

Yes, walked out, en masse.

The particular group had been a hard sell from day one. The mix included more outspoken individuals than usual, many from difficult situations, and the bitterness to prove it.

I finished the first topic of the morning and dismissed the group for a coffee break. Our staff room overlooked the parking lot and I observed four who smoked leaning against a perimeter fence. The fifteen minutes ended and I returned to the room where half the people had returned. Then I waited, giving people a couple minutes latitude before resuming. And we waited. Eventually I began, annoyed that the missing participants would soon interrupt us.

Fully twenty minutes in Richard leaned back in his chair and glanced out the window. "Oh man," he blurted out, "Debbie is being frisked!"

"What?" the chorus followed.

"Yeah, the police have her pinned against the wall and they're taking Ralph's wallet from him."

With that, Leona shot into the room. "You guys won't believe what's happening out there. We watched this jerk hit an old lady's car and then try to leave. Debbie ran over and banged on his window and Ralph stood right in front of his car so he couldn't get away. The guy got out and started screaming and pushed Debbie and she shoved him back. Someone called the cops and now the cop is busting up Debbie, like she's the bad guy here." Leona turned to leave.

> *"Oh man," he blurted out, "Debbie is being frisked!"*

"Whoa, Leona, slow down. Are the police asking you to go back down?"

"No, I just want to see what happens!"

"Why don't you just have a seat and let the police deal with it. They don't need extra observers…"

"Are you kidding me?" Leona interrupted, "And miss all this action? No way! Come on you guys," she motioned to the others.

"No, we definitely don't…" But none of them heard me. They were too busy leaving.

In the end Debbie didn't go to jail and after everyone returned we spent the remainder of our time debriefing the event and exploring alternate approaches to the police incident. And while the twist on the day certainly entertained, it never felt as perilous as some of our other client experiences.

My boss prioritized safety and routinely reminded us that if ever we felt in danger or in need of an out with a difficult client, we could say: "Company policy doesn't allow us to do that. If you'd like to take it up with the owner, I can help you make an appointment with him."

Our receptionist used this line with the male client whose attention went from loitering at the counter to bringing flowers to asking her on a walk in his favorite park. I took the same out with the man who shifted talk from his resume to the new motorcycle he bought and how he'd like to give me a ride.

But no day was I more grateful for my boss' protective spirit than when I met with Larry for his follow-up appointment.

Larry had engaged in class discussion sporadically but preferred to linger after class to ask his questions. His work history showed gaps and his poor hygiene made me wonder what else was going on for him. I felt unsure what to expect at his scheduled coaching appointment.

We discussed interviewing, with no red flags, so I began to close, "Do you have anything else you'd like to ask me about?"

"Yeah, actually I do. Last month I went to Las Vegas for the weekend and met a woman." In seconds, graphic details of a bizarre sexual encounter poured out. I sat speechless, stunned by the wild topic shift and shocked by his request that I be his sex advisor. After too long, I stood and stammered, "Actually, our company policy doesn't allow...."

Larry never made an appointment with my boss and we staff took the incident as a reminder to remain vigilant in watching out for one another and making sure we never let a client get between us and our escape route! Our goal for clients to experience a safe learning environment had to begin with taking care of ourselves.

**CAN'T YOU JUST HIRE ME?**

# "I Hate Animals!"

An uneasy silence filled the room as participants arrived for the first of two days on interview skills. Something about this topic quieted the crowd each month. I took my place and began with an attempt to put them at ease.

"Good morning. Let's start with imagining yourself as the boss in charge of hiring a new receptionist – the first person a customer will see when they enter your business. An applicant, Sarah, is shown to the interviewee chair and you are about to determine if she is the right fit for the job. As you glance up from your notes, Sarah greets you with a warm grin. There, hanging front and center from her top teeth, is a chunk of leafy green something-or-other. What do you do?"

"Thank God it's not me!" shouted Bernie.

"I'd probably burst out laughing," added Amanda, "which I realize isn't very nice but…"

Cara interrupted, "I'd just look at her and ask, 'So, how'd you enjoy your lunch?'"

I think that's my favorite answer ever for that scenario. Once we composed ourselves and enjoyed the pressure relief,

I asked what they thought the purpose of my question had been.

Amanda responded first. "I suspect you want us to check our teeth before we go to our own appointments."

"Good idea! And let's begin thinking about small things that can make a big statement in creating impressions. Do you know that an interviewer's initial sense of you is formed within seconds of meeting? Obviously an impression can be changed over time but those first ones are powerful. So, how are we going to make the most of those early minutes? Let's think about how we look first."

Bernie shook his head vehemently. "No way. You're not going to get me wearing some three-piece monkey suit to an interview!"

"No, I'm definitely not going to ask you to wear a suit to a construction site. You'd likely get laughed off the lot! But what would you wear?"

> *"You're not going to get me wearing some three-piece monkey suit to an interview!"*

"Clean jeans, a golf shirt and I'd have my work boots and tool belt in my truck in case they want me to swing a hammer for the day and see what I can do."

"And is it fair to say that those clothes are one notch dressier than your regular work wear?" Bernie nodded. "That's the general rule when putting together an outfit for your interview. Do your research on dress code in that environment and then dress a bit better than the norm."

"And do make sure your clothing is clean, appropriate and in good repair. I had a candidate come for an interview once dressed in four-inch stiletto heels. She leaned on the reception counter (don't do that, by the way!) and nervously fidgeted her feet. Somehow she managed to rock back and snap off a heel. Her entry into my office a few minutes later had a distinct 'step, thunk, step, thunk'. She was off her game when it came to answering questions."

"Oh, I can top that story!" Cara, a well-endowed 40-something woman began telling of her appointment to discuss a reception position with a manufacturing company. "I had a hard time deciding what to wear because I've put on a few pounds since I lost my job. In the end, I went with a white blouse and navy pants. I thought they looked okay."

"That sounds like a good choice for the position you've described," I affirmed.

"Yeah, maybe. It was two guys interviewing me and I thought I answered the first questions well but they kept giving each other these weird looks. And the creepiest thing happened – I caught them looking at my boobs!"

"What?" exclaimed Amanda. "Are you serious? And you didn't just get up and walk out? I wouldn't want to work for someone like that!"

Cara continued. "That's what I was thinking as the appointment went on. I was so mad by the time I left. All the way to my car I kicked myself for not confronting them or storming out. I was so upset I dropped my purse by the car door and as I bent over to pick it up I was horrified to see that my blouse was gaping open right at my chest with gorgeous lacy bra for the world to see!"

We collectively gasped as Cara nodded. "Yup, I sat through the whole interview exposing more than my work skills!"

"Oh Cara, it feels like we shouldn't be laughing but you tell a great story! So what did you do?" I inquired.

"I thought about calling and apologizing. I thought about going back, properly dressed. In the end, I decided to chalk it up as a lesson and left it. Oh, but I did go shopping and bought a sweater with no buttons for the next round!"

"Good call. I don't think I've ever heard a better reason to make sure your attire is in proper shape. In fact, I would like you all to come to class tomorrow dressed like you would for an interview. The point of the exercise is not to inspect your clothing but rather to encourage you to have an outfit assembled that fits, is seasonal and appropriate for your industry. Then, when you get the call, you're ready."

We wrapped up the discussion on how to dress and spent a few minutes talking about having fresh breath, not smelling like smoke, avoiding perfumed products – it's never a great sell if your interviewer is allergic to you – and turning cell phones off. Then we moved on to arriving at the company.

"Who will be your first point of contact when you show up for your appointment?" I asked.

The group replied in unison, "The receptionist."

"Exactly. And a mistake we often make is interacting with the receptionist as if he or she is not part of the hiring process. I've heard of big city companies who ask the doorman how a candidate treated him. Everyone you come in contact with could be in on making the decision. Let me give you an example of why this is so important."

I described Marilyn to the class, a previous client who had shared her story with me. Marilyn arrived thirty minutes early for a sales position interview at a pet supply company. The receptionist had motioned her to wait in the lobby and returned to her work but Marilyn, being nervous and chatty, started talking at her. Marilyn told of past work and her family's current decision to get rid of their dog. She went into detail describing her hatred for the "beast" and her wanting him to be gone. She even added that no animal would ever be welcome in her home again.

I asked the class, "Do any of you recall what I said she was there for?"

"A sales position, I think," answered Bernie.

"Yes, at a pet supply company!" I added.

"Oh no, this is not going to end well, is it?" Amanda went on. "I'm willing to bet she didn't get the job."

"In fact, Marilyn didn't even get the interview! When the hiring manager came to call her in, the receptionist took him aside. After their exchange, he approached Marilyn and said, 'Julie tells me you hate animals so I'm going to save your time and mine. We're a pet supply company and we need animal lovers.'"

"Oh, ouch!" Bernie exclaimed. "That's harsh."

"And the moral of the story is...consider everyone at the interview location a part of the decision-making team. You never know the influence someone has. With that in mind it's time to practice interacting with a front line person. What will be important?"

The group brainstormed and agreed that arriving at the building 15-20 minutes early would give time to settle oneself but not going into the actual office more than 5-10 minutes ahead made sense. Once inside, making eye contact with the receptionist, smiling and not flopping arms or papers or purse on the counter mattered.

"A confident, friendly interaction might sound like this: 'Hi, my name is Shelaine Strom and I am here for an interview with Bob Smith at 10:15.' Simple and straight forward, but requiring practice."

> *"My name is Sandra Green and I'm here for an interview at 10:60."*

"Seriously? You're going to make us practice saying who we are?" Bernie looked more nervous than irritated.

"I can't tell you how many times I've had people in mock and real situations walk in and forget the interviewer's name or even their own. My all-time favorite was the client – in a practice situation – who came up to the front desk and said, 'My name is Sandra Green and I'm here for an interview at 10:60.' Our receptionist politely responded, 'Would that be 11:00?' at which point they both burst out laughing. So much for staying in character!"

The class moved through the exercise of conversing with the receptionist and put together ways to respond and market themselves to potential employers. After working diligently on answers to a set of questions, Bernie's frustration surfaced.

"I really don't see the point in doing this. Who really asks someone to 'Tell me a little bit about yourself?'"

Amanda responded to Bernie immediately, "Every interview I've had started that way! And every time I felt like a deer in the headlights – not to mention I see now how awful my answers were. I totally thought they wanted personal information. This format you've given us really helps – share a brief summary of past experiences and successes, talk about skills and abilities and then say what I'm looking for now. It's my professional self."

"I find it's helpful to follow that pattern, Amanda. And Bernie, I appreciate you questioning this. In the construction industry you've probably had fewer formal interviews. That said, there are companies that use these questions and it never hurts to be prepared. Amanda, your experience is common as well. In fact, we had a client once call us immediately after an interview – with an irritated manner – to say that his interviewer used this exact list! He had been a skeptic all through class so we weren't sure if he was upset with that company's lack of creativity or that he had to admit we knew our stuff."

Cara weighed in. "I can see why it's important to prepare, so I have my skills in mind and specific examples ready to share. But what do we do about the unpredictable things – like my clothing malfunction?"

"Fair enough. Interviews will most often have that element of the unknown, so it's good to prepare by having someone practice with you and shoot you a variety of questions. And keep in mind your response to the unexpected is an opportunity to show character as well. We aren't looking for perfection. Let me tell you about Tim."

"A few years prior, I worked as Director of Personnel on a board and participated in many hiring interviews. Tim arrived for his turn and I greeted this exuberant young man, chatting with him as I showed him to the board room.

I motioned him to a chair, gave him a glass of water and moved the box of Kleenex within his reach.

When the CEO of the company entered the room Tim shot up and enthusiastically thrust out his arm to shake hands. Unfortunately that glass of water sat directly in the line of fire.

"Oh no," cringed Amanda.

"Oh yes," I continued. "And to say he spilled the water doesn't do justice. He launched it! The force of the glass hitting the table sent a geyser straight up onto the CEO's tie, glasses, hair. We all gaped, and then our CEO chuckled and said, 'Well, that's a first' and left to towel down."

"The poor guy!" Amanda sympathized.

"Who? Tim or the CEO?" teased Bernie. "I wouldn't want to be either. So what happened?"

"We proceeded with the interview and were thoroughly impressed with the young man's resilience. He apologized appropriately and showed an ability to laugh at himself without beating up himself. Later he humorously wove his blunder into an answer about dealing with stressful situations. In the end, we hired him."

Amanda shook her head in disbelief. "I think I would drop to my belly on the floor and slink out, hoping to never see these people again."

"And that would be a first as well!" I joked. "But keep in mind the goal is to demonstrate your genuine self, not an unrealistic perfect self. Interviewers know you're nervous and they're human too! They likely had to sit through an interview to get where they are. So for now, let's get back to working on your answers so you'll be ready for a day of practicing tomorrow."

# A Bikini and a Little Black Dress

The second day on interview skills generated more apprehension. People arrived late offering excuses from "I really didn't want to come" to "I couldn't figure out my outfit" and even "I couldn't get out of the bathroom!" Clearly even mock interviews created stress.

Eleanor, however, a sixty-two-year-old who usually came in her gardening grubs broke from the norm. She appeared at 8:57 a.m. wearing an Armani suit, strutting Prada shoes and flashing a Gucci bag. Her ensemble included meticulously coiffed hair and business-professional makeup. I hardly recognized her.

Once my antsy audience was seated I reviewed the principles from the previous day and asked for success stories where interviews secured jobs. Eleanor volunteered immediately.

"Many years ago, I was told to meet a man in the parking lot behind the Bernard building at 8:00 a.m. the next day and to bring a bikini and a cocktail dress." The class members gasped and one dared ask, "No way! So what did you do?"

Eleanor replied, reveling in shock value, "I met him in the parking lot and took a bikini and a little black dress, of course!"

Group faces ranged from stunned to horrified. "He arrived in his limo, introduced himself and asked if I was available until midnight. I got in the car and we drove to his beach house. I met his wife and children and spent the day on the shore – yes, in my bikini – playing with their five year-old boy and three year-old girl. Late in the afternoon, as instructed, I brought them in and got them ready for a dinner party and, you guessed it, put on my dress. These parents liked their children to be included in events and also wanted freedom to mingle with their guests. I watched the children, put them to bed and the limo driver had me back to the parking lot by midnight, as promised." Eleanor punctuated her story with a smug smile.

> *"I met him in the parking lot and took a bikini and a little black dress, of course!"*

"And that was it?" ventured Julie, unable to contain her curiosity.

"Oh no, I was hired and worked for the couple for six years. You'd know them if I told you their names. They're famous Hollywood actors."

It's hard to know in moments like those what to believe. Introduce the topic of job interviews and the tales of tragedy, hilarity, embarrassment and triumph get told. It wasn't my job to assess the accuracy of the accounts and they certainly entertained and provided colorful teaching illustrations.

"Wow, that's quite the story. I'm glad to hear it turned out well for you, Eleanor. And it also brings up the issue of safety during this process. I must admit, it did alarm me that you got into a car with a stranger who asked you to bring a bathing suit!"

"Well," Eleanor conceded, "I did leave a few pieces out – for dramatic effect. I was referred by a friend and I knew who the couple was ahead of time." Her classmates looked relieved and then unimpressed.

Leah spoke up. "I think safety is a big deal. I went for an interview once presumably at a retail outlet. It was an empty showroom with only one guy there telling me we'd have our 'chat' in the backroom. I got out of there as fast as I could."

"Good for you, Leah. It's so important that we trust our inner red flags and protect ourselves."

Janet jumped in. "But it isn't just about physical safety. There's a ton of scam artists out there. I got called for an interview and when I showed up, there were about 20 of us. A 'select few' of us got called back for the 'amazing opportunity' only to find out I'd have to shell out 500 bucks to buy the starter sales kit. I left, too."

Cindy spoke up. "I was so excited when I got called for an interview with an investment and development company. The position met all my criteria – close to home, using my administrative skills, great pay. I wanted to nail this job so I put hours into researching but the more I dug, the more I smelled a scam. Long story short, I went to the police and they sent me into the interview undercover. My testimony cracked open an investment fraud case which led to arrests and convictions."

"Guess you didn't get that job, hey?" chided Eleanor.

I weighed in. "Those are clear examples of how important it is to be safe and do our homework ahead of time. In most situations our research will not be about court cases but will give us insights on the company and help us present ourselves well. So, let's assume we've researched the company and now we're going to prepare answers for specific questions."

We considered the book *Acing the Interview: How to Ask and Answer the Questions that Will Get You the Job* that suggests an employer needs four big-picture questions answered to feel confident about a hire.[2] Firstly, they want to know, "Can you do the job?" This addresses skills and past experience. Secondly, they consider, "Do I/we like you?" Or, is your personality a fit to the workplace culture or team? Thirdly, "Are you a risk?" which really means how big a risk? In other words, will hiring you cost me money, time, or reputation? And finally, "Can we work the money out?"

With those ideas as the backdrop, we took on a classic question employers love to ask – "What is one of your greatest weaknesses?"

"I hate that question!" Janet declared boldly.

"You're not alone. Let's break it down and figure out how to respond effectively. First of all, what does the employer really want to know?" Participants thought it primarily addressed risk assessment and from there we brainstormed how to respond.

"A solid answer needs to be honest and not canned or cheesy like, 'my biggest weakness is really my greatest strength.' In fact, when my boss gets an answer like that he counters with, 'Okay, but I want to know what you're really lousy at.' It also needs to show self-awareness and gives you opportunity to illustrate problem solving skills and how willing you are to learn and grow. And, perhaps most important to the employer, you can show that you're a risk worth taking.

Whatever is asked, you need to identify the question behind the question and address the employer's unspoken concern. Also, giving real life examples of skill-use in concise story form gives a company tangible material to assess. It's the 'show, don't tell' approach. For example, you might be asked 'What motivates you?' An answer for a retail customer service position could be: 'In my previous positions, I made listening carefully to my customer's need a high priority. I asked questions to clarify what they really wanted and made every effort to match their need to our product. I had a strong repeat-customer base, my manager asked me to train new staff in shopper-care and I had a great sense of personal satisfaction in helping people.'

*"You need to identify the question behind the question and address the employer's unspoken concern."*

In this example, a retail owner's underlying concern could be related to assessing risk. This candidate shows a value for customer care and an ability to secure repeat business – both key to thriving in retail. In addition, evidence of previous customer service work is present and responsibility and training skills are highlighted. This interviewee could be well on his way to landing a job if he demonstrates other skills and experiences similarly throughout the interview."

After discussing this example, people worked diligently documenting personal skills and experiences that matched positions of interest. We were ready to practice.

As I prepared the group for the mock interviews I requested that they show me how they planned to sit. I scanned the room, seeing twelve individuals pulling themselves into a more intentional posture. "Great. We're looking for something between slouching and the airplane mode of 'full, upright, locked position.' Putting both feet on the floor or crossing your ankles can be helpful, especially if you're a foot tapper. And watch out for distracting behavior like jingling keys in your pocket or repeatedly clicking a pen. The goal is to not annoy the interviewer."

I carried on with the significance of non-verbal behavior including the power of a firm and confident handshake (but not a bone-crushing one), and good eye contact.

"I interviewed a woman once who spent the entire time looking about one inch over my head. It created the oddest feeling – like I should rise out of my seat to meet her gaze. And don't be like the man who stared like a zombie or the guy who cased the room as if he intended to rob the place after hours."

Eleanor shook her head and asked, "Do you stay awake at night making this stuff up?"

"No," I smiled, "I've seen it all and had a few disasters of my own as an interviewee. One interview, early in my career, was for a social work position. I had prepared thoroughly but felt nervous. As I sat through the session, my stress began to take physical form in leg tremors. They became so intense I couldn't rest my hands on my thighs without my upper body shaking. So there I sat, hands hovering inches above my lap, trying to recall details of the Child Protection Act! Not the best."

Janet waved her arm in the air. "That's me. I tremble too! So how do you control it?"

"Somewhere along the line I learned a simple technique that works great for me. First is to recognize it's happening and then start a conversation with yourself. *'I'm obviously stressed. What's going on?'* Then I breathe deeply and try to 'talk myself off the ledge.' If that's not enough then I use muscle relaxation. Start with your toes – tense them and then relax them. Then tense both of your feet and slowly work your way up your body, tightening and then relaxing your muscles. They can't shake if they are doing this."

"How far up your body do you go?" laughed Eleanor. "I'm picturing you in an interview scrunching your shoulders into your ears and then pinching your face up all tight."

I chuckled, "Yeah, maybe not that far! I suppose it could be entertaining for the interviewer but that's really not my goal. If you stop at your waist no one will be onto you. It does work. I use it here in class when discussions get intense. Bet you never knew."

The remainder of the day included multiple opportunities to practice with each person playing the role of interviewer, observer and candidate. We reconvened as a large group and I began the debriefing.

"Here's how I'd like to end our day. Please tell me two areas you feel you have improved on or learned something about in these two interview days. Leah, would you be willing to start?"

"When you told us we would have to practice interviews today, I felt sick to my stomach. So, I guess one positive outcome is that I didn't throw up! No, seriously, I was that nervous. And the second would be that I actually had something to say and didn't just go blank."

We went around the room hearing how confidence increased, eye contact improved, fidgeting lessened, but perhaps the best summary of all came from Janet when she volunteered, "I had no idea how much practice could help!"

## The Wordless Interview

"He's a quiet client," my fellow instructor told me. "And only three people are in the class this month."

A typical class was twelve but I had learned that numbers ebbed and flowed for reasons beyond understanding. All I knew was that these particular people were here for this particular session at this particular point in their lives and we would do our best to offer them a positive experience.

I responded to that effect and predicted that Jack would likely come out of his shell. My co-worker contorted her face, "No, he's *really* quiet!"

"*Really* quiet? What do you mean?"

"Well, he doesn't speak at all."

"Do you mean he physically can't speak?"

"No. He can, but he likely won't. At all. Ever." She seemed convinced. I wasn't.

Lots of people came into our program depressed, lacking self-confidence or nervous about entering a new group. I had met all kinds and felt confident that we offered clients a safe place to process their job transition. I had years of practice asking questions, gently probing and encouraging individuals to share their thoughts and experiences. I loved the challenge and proceeded undaunted by the prospect of one third of my group being speechless.

I soon discovered that Jack was in fact different from most depressed or shy clients. I'd ask a general question and the group would be silent. I'd wait for answers, being sure to allow time for him to work up courage. Often Linda would speak up and then Kurt would add a thought or two.

Not Jack. He remained committed to his non-verbal position, only periodically lifting his eyes or nodding in agreement, assuring me that he was still with us. I resolved that whatever he could take in, he would, and that out of respect for whatever his unknown story was, I would leave him in peace – and quiet.

*I had yet to teach someone how to navigate interviewing without speaking.*

But then it occurred to me that we would be addressing interview skills and I had yet to teach someone how to navigate interviewing without speaking. Much class content revolved around creating answers to common interview questions and practicing them with each other – out loud, using words. I pondered options the night before. Jack could be the observer and carry on with his wordless presence. Maybe he would be willing to write comments. I could push him a little but would he be overwhelmed and leave the program? That's not the result I desired.

I settled on where I often ended up. I would let go of the outcome, and if past experiences taught me anything, the end likely wouldn't look like anything I could have predicted.

Interview day came and Linda, Kurt and Jack arrived on time. I gave my introduction, working hard to address the anxieties that plague interviewees.

"You are not alone if you feel nervous," I assured. "Interviews are unlike most of life so feeling uncomfortable makes sense. And please keep in mind; no one has ever died of an interview!" My two talkers smiled and then turned away, distracted by the quietest giggle coming from Jack's corner. I looked over to see Jack holding his hand over his mouth.

I returned a grin and he snickered. We three others joined in. His snicker became a chuckle, then a chortle and before we knew it, he was engaged in full blown uproarious laughter. Stunned by his private hilarity, we stared in wonder at what had struck him so funny. Gasping for air and face fully red, he put his head on the table, slapped his hand down repeatedly and continued his solitary amusement. We watched and smiled and laughed and began moving to that awkward place on the outside of an inside joke. Linda and Kurt asked what was funny. Not surprisingly, but now for reason of joviality, he didn't answer. He could not answer.

No longer able to contain himself, he pushed away from the table, stood up only to double over, and stumbled down the hall, past reception and out the door.

Now we were the silent ones. Dumbfounded, really. The face of Amy poking into the classroom broke our stupor. "What was that about?" she asked, to which we raised our hands with "no clue!"

I stumbled through a couple more interactions and tried to reorient myself to the topic wondering if we'd see Jack again and the additional disappointing thought – would we ever know what he found so gut-bustingly funny?

At least fifteen minutes passed when I heard the bell on the entry door jingle signaling that perhaps Jack was returning. Sure enough, he slipped in through the door and back to his place. I paused, debating if it was worth asking, but Linda and Kurt blurted, "What was that about?"

Jack started to giggle and appeared as if he would repeat the comic scene. He grabbed the edge of the table as he took two slow deep breaths and spoke.

"No one ever died of an interview but I did faint at one once." His laughter resumed as we joined with him.

"Seriously, you fainted at a job interview?" Linda searched.

"I was really nervous. The room started to spin and went black. I woke up on the floor. I didn't get the job."

"But you lived to tell about it!" I added.

"Yeah, and I did get another job not too long after that. I worked there until they shut down a year ago."

And so it went. Jack certainly did not hog the floor after that day, but he participated – with words. We learned more of his story, one including brain surgery and his long journey back to using limbs and language, functions he once took for granted. By the end of the program he acknowledged feeling safe, heard, and more self-confident in his offerings and I was reminded of the value of each person's story and the privilege of hearing it.

# WHAT SHOULD I BE WHEN I GROW UP?

# The Chaos Theory of Squirrels

"We are going to start our day with a coloring project," I explained. "You will each receive a box of crayons and a picture. Please don't begin coloring until everyone has materials and I've given instructions."

"I love coloring!" Aisha squealed. But Boyd mocked, "Oh goody, I'll have a picture for my fridge tonight. I can tell my kids, 'This is what daddy did at school today.'"

"Your kids will be so proud," I replied with a smile and began the directions. "There is only one rule for this exercise. Please color the picture, disregarding the lines."

"What?" questioned Cassandra, a middle-aged woman recently let go from a bookkeeping position. "That's impossible. What do you mean by that?"

"There's no trick. I'm simply asking you to color the picture you have before you disregarding the lines." The group sat silently, some staring at the paper, others glaring at me.

Aisha picked up the crayon box and dumped the contents before her. She worked intently, alternating colors and checking with her neighbors to see if they had other shades she could borrow.

Boyd's box sat unopened right where I had placed it and his sheet remained unmarked. He picked up his book and began to read.

Cassandra held a crayon in hand but made no motion toward the paper. "This isn't right. You can't color properly if you don't pay attention to the lines. Lines are there for a reason – they are meant to be colored in."

Irene added, "My teachers always said it was important to be careful and color inside the lines. That's what I've always tried to do. Are you sure you want me to pretend they aren't there?"

"Yes, I am asking you to disregard the lines, Irene." She furrowed her brow and gave me a reluctant, "Okay, if you say so."

I gave the group another five minutes to finish the project and then asked them to hold up their paper for me and the rest of the group to see.

"Oh great, now it's show and tell time," Boyd scoffed.

"Yes, it is. Would you all please take a look around at each other's work? What do you see?"

Cassandra gaped at Aisha's page. "What on earth? You just colored a giant rainbow over top of everything."

Aisha beamed. "I sure did and it was so much fun!" to which Cassandra shook her head in disbelief.

*"What on earth? you just colored a giant rainbow over top of everything."*

We spent a few minutes enjoying the artistic expressions of the activity and then I posed the question. "I'd like you to think back to that first moment I gave you the directions about ignoring the lines. What were you thinking? How did you feel?"

The group offered a range from frustration, disgust and anger to delight, freedom and fun.

"Wow, that's quite the spectrum isn't it? And all of that attached to a simple request that you color outside the lines. We could spend hours looking at how each of you, according to your personal style alone, responded to the exercise," I suggested.

"What do you mean by that?" asked Cassandra.

"Well, let's do a quick overview. Boyd has a blank page. Why is that, Boyd?" I inquired.

"Because it was a waste of my time," he replied sharply.

"Remember how Behaviorals are task oriented and want efficiency? And you weren't worried about hurting my feelings, were you?"

"No. Why would I be? You're a big girl."

I nodded and carried on with Cognitives reviewing how this style values things done the right way by paying close attention to detail. "Take a look at Cassandra's picture. See the meticulous care put into coloring right up to the edge of each line but it's all within the lines."

Cassandra took offense. "It is not!"

I was taken aback by her intensity. "Oh, I'm sorry. Am I missing something from over here?"

Cassandra slid her picture in front of her neighbor and pointed to one spot on the page. "See. Right there."

Irene strained down at the page. "What am I looking for, exactly?"

Cassandra grew impatient. "Right there. I went over the line right *there!*" Sure enough, on close inspection, one could see a tiny mark outside the black outline. Cassandra explained the internal tension the exercise created. Years of belief that coloring correctly – staying inside the lines – was pitted against my rule which she also wanted to obey. Her compromise was one small deviation.

"And Irene, how about your experience?"

She replied. "I found this very hard. I could hear all of my elementary school teachers' voices telling me how to color properly and then your voice saying to do the opposite. I felt like I had to choose who to disappoint."

"Interpersonals do care about pleasing others and not causing conflict. And from your picture it would seem that you did what I asked. Am I correct?" Irene held up her picture showing a page divided into three vertical color blocks.

"I really didn't know what to do at first and then I saw Aisha doing her rainbow. That gave me the idea. Once I started and knew that others were doing it too, I kind of enjoyed it. I really like coloring."

Aisha jumped in before I could transition to an explanation of her style. "I loved this exercise. You gave me freedom to do whatever creative thing I wanted to. I find lines constraining. Give me blank pages and let me go!" The class laughed as Aisha spread her arms and threatened to take flight.

"There you have the summary of Aisha's style. Affectives love creativity, freedom and the opportunity to influence others. See how style reveals itself over and over?" I asked.

"Yup. Got it. So what's the point of coloring?" Boyd asked impatiently.

"We are talking about career decision making today – the 'what do you want to be when you grow up' portion of this class. In a small way this exercise may give you a window into why you respond the way you do to this process. In other words, figuring out your next career move can involve a lot of coloring outside the lines."

I went on to describe how career satisfaction connects with finding work consistent with one's values, skills and interests. We enjoy our jobs more if they fit well with our identity.

> *"Figuring out your next career move can involve a lot of coloring outside the lines."*

"It seems like common sense, doesn't it?" I asked. "But over and over again I see people who haven't taken time or had opportunity to consider values, skills and interests as they relate to work life. The more you understand yourself and career opportunities, the more likely you will find a match and enjoy greater job fulfillment."

I went on to explain one of my favorite career development models by career counsellor and author Jim Bright – The Chaos Theory.[3]

"Well, chaos certainly describes how my life feels right now," whispered Irene.

"And in that comment I think I hear some of the stress that comes with life feeling out of control. That is certainly part of this approach. I like how Jim Bright describes our career path as not being a straight line. He says, '…sometimes small steps have profound outcomes, and sometimes changing everything changes nothing.' Believe it or not, squirrels have given me a living picture of what this means." I told this story.

"The squirrels in my backyard have a travel route between our neighbor's fence and a hazelnut tree on the opposite side of our property.

One little black squirrel's navigational choices intrigued me. He launched himself from our shed roof into the cherry tree and started down one branch, only to hop up a level and carry on. He backtracked and jumped down two branches. He headed straight up the tree trunk, gaining ten feet of elevation but made no forward progress. He advanced on such a tiny twig that it drooped and swayed under his weight. He jumped to a sturdier limb nearby.

Eventually my little friend (who I have named Coal) arrived in the hazelnut tree and happily filled his cheeks."

"Great," interjected Boyd. "Now we've gone from coloring like kids to tree-hopping like squirrels."

"Bear with me. When we're in career transition, we probably envision a destination – like the squirrel eyeing the tree – or at least a general idea of a good job. We start down an internet research 'branch' and it becomes weak so we jump to another one – say, networking. We're still moving, still seeing our 'end tree,' but now feeling overwhelmed so we rest and collect ourselves regarding next steps – our shed roof equivalent.

And the next step is critical for a squirrel. To look only at the hazelnut tree and not where your little paw is putting down could be disastrous! I also observed that Coal found many treasures along the way by paying attention to his present environment. Similarly, in a career journey you may bump into unexpected delights. For example my co-worker Ann came to our program as a client and has never left. She had no idea that first step would lead to seven years of employment."

"So you're offering us all jobs? Is that the point?" jabbed Boyd.

"Not quite. But I am curious if you have networked with everyone here, and after this program will we know what you're looking for?"

Boyd shook his head.

"Just like my squirrel that took flying leaps and had to scramble to safety we need to get out of our comfort zone and ask people for leads and connections. And keep in mind what Bright said, some significant moves we make will result in nothing, but some tiny steps can have profound outcomes."

"I feel exhausted just hearing about your poor little squirrel going miles to get across your yard. I need to know. Did he ever make it?" Irene questioned hopefully.

"Yes, Coal did make it. He gathered his prize but – and here's another application to our world – he didn't set up permanent shop. He didn't make the tree his home nor invest everything in that one location. He enjoyed it. He stocked up and took in all that he could and when it was time, he moved on."

Irene gave me an "I don't like where this is going" look.

"Irene, I'm wondering if your 'company loyalty' button is being pushed, because some of us – shall I say, more mature workers – have the belief that we work as a faithful employee, the company takes care of us, and we receive the 'gold watch' at 65 when they throw us a retirement party."

Irene nodded enthusiastically.

"I regret to inform you – and need to regularly remind myself – those days are gone. Today's work world requires the squirrel's attitude. We must consider a job a destination for a time, not a home. A job is both an opportunity to contribute to an organization and a chance to gather more skills and abilities. It's a means of growing and learning and adding gear to your tool box."

"Oh I find that stressful even to consider," admitted Cassandra. "I like having a plan, steps to accomplishing it, and believing it will lead to something permanent. I really hate change."

"And that's why we are having this conversation – to help you identify your expectations and see where you're likely to hit roadblocks. If you can name your fears or dead ends, then you can create a plan to address and overcome them."

"Not me!" Aisha burst in, "I'm going to take the Coal approach and go every which way. That sounds like more fun!"

We ended our discussion with this idea that a job is a temporary stopping place, some for six months, others six years, and some longer still. We need to develop the mindset of a lifelong learner who seeks new opportunities and is willing to risk jumping to a new branch. We can work on being resilient people, ones who can weather change, or – to carry on the metaphor – ones who can fall out of the tree, pick ourselves up, take care of injuries from the plunge, know our bigger vision and begin navigating again, from branch to branch toward our goal.

## Grandpa's Scree Sifter

Know yourself, know your career. It's a phrase I return to when walking with someone through career decision-making. In so few words it represents much self-awareness and more decisions.

I posed the question, "Have you ever done a Google search on a topic and received two million possibilities?" The class laughed, and Robert, a particularly detail-oriented client, sighed and added, "That's when I feel so overwhelmed. I don't know where to start – so I just don't." Others nodded, affirming his distress.

I began to tell a story. "A very special treat for me as a five year-old was to accompany my grandfather to his work site. He worked as a stone mason – someone who crafted rock into fireplaces and cairns. One of his tools was a large wooden frame overlaid with sturdy wire mesh. He would shovel rock and gravel onto the screen and I would 'help' him shake it until only the big rocks remained. I imitated his every action, picking up and examining each stone for its suitability to the project."

Al chimed in, impatience oozing, "So, he lessened his workload and saved time by running his options through a sieve. I get that. But how does that relate to a million internet hits or hundreds of possible training options I can choose?"

"It's the same principle. If you create a filter for your ideal vocation, then any job or education possibility you find can be run through it. You save time and energy because you've already made some decisions. So let's talk about what your filter will include."

I drew a large funnel on the flip chart and we brainstormed together. "If you think about having an ideal work situation, what matters to you? What would be important?"

*"If you think about having an ideal work situation, what matters to you?"*

"I would have to work with people. I can't stand being shut away in an office," to which another participant responded, "Not me! I don't really like people. Just give me a computer and let me do my work."

I drew a line on the funnel and wrote *personality style*. "Whatever your particular bent, it's important that the job requirements match your natural strengths. What else makes a job meaningful for you?"

Al noted, "I like to work in a community different from where I live. My job involves a lot of confidential interaction and I don't like running into clients in the grocery store." Several others added that working close to home would be their ideal.

"So *location* of work matters." I added it to the flip chart.

"Pay matters to me!" threw out Robert.

"Let's talk about pay. Have you calculated how much it costs you to maintain your current standard of living – assuming that's your goal? How much will you need to make? If the job includes benefits would that decrease the hourly amount you need to earn? Are you willing to relocate in order to make a higher wage? These are some of the questions we need to ask ourselves in order to determine our target salary." *Income* became the third line of the filter.

The class agreed the fourth layer would be *hours* – some wanting full-time, some part-time, some only during school hours, and some willing to do shift work. The variety of preferences ranged greatly as layers continued to be added.

"I want to be the boss," Ken announced, to which Emily replied, "Go right ahead! I hate being in charge. Just give me my tasks and let me do my work but please don't micromanage me!" I wrote down *level of responsibility* and *degree of freedom/supervision*.

We included a few additional ideas and I summarized: "What we're really getting at with this exercise is clarifying what you value in a work context. I would encourage you to go through each of these categories and ask yourself what is *your* particular value, need or want. When a job possibility comes along you can run it through your filter and see how it lines up with your values."

I continued. "Many good hits that cross your path will be excluded easily when they don't meet the criteria you've set out. What you're really doing is pre-deciding how you'll spend time doing further investigating."

"Okay, but what if I run three jobs through my filter and two of them meet my criteria about equally? Then what do I do?" queried Robert.

"Maybe you've heard of the 'make a list of pros and cons' approach. That can be insightful as you visually assess what's a plus or minus. It can also be helpful to ask for the perspective of someone you trust—assuming you welcome their reasoning and are open to choosing something different!" I smiled as some processed the challenge of not taking certain people's advice.

"Here's another approach you may not have encountered. Let's call it 'sitting with a decision.' Say you are trying to decide whether or not to go back to school. For one day, live and think and act as if you are going to school. Change your language to 'I am doing this' instead of 'I might do this', even if it's just in your head. As you go through this day, pay attention to your whole being. How does your body feel – muscles, heart, stomach, head? What thoughts come to mind? Where did your feelings take you? If you can, write down what you experienced at the end of the day.

The next day do the same exercise but this time act as if you are not going back to school and, once again, pay attention to your internal responses. If this isn't the best decision for you, you may experience tensed muscles, sadness, racing heart, diarrhea, anxiety, or headache. If we clarify our values, run options through that filter, assess the positives and negatives of choices and we spend time deliberately paying attention to our inner selves, added all together, most often the direction will be clearer."

Robert's face tensed, "But what if I make the wrong decision?"

"That fear can paralyze us from making decisions, so I wonder if we can think differently about that. Consider your last job. If you set aside the ending of it for a minute, did you learn anything while you were there?"

Emily offered, "Well, I guess so. When they hired me I had never worked on a computer before. Now I can use several programs and I'm actually pretty good at data entry."

"Anything else, Emily?"

"I have lots of industry knowledge now. And, like I mentioned before, I sure learned that I don't want to work for a micromanager!" The class resoundingly agreed.

"And that's what I mean about changing our thinking around decision-making. It's impossible to know all the potential outcomes of any decision. But rather than dwelling on a 'wrong' decision, can we think in terms of gain and development? Are you willing to see life – full of all its decisions – as one long opportunity to learn and grow?"

*"Are you willing to see life – full of all its decisions – as one long opportunity to learn and grow?"*

Robert interjected with a cheeky smile, "Sometimes I think it's better to sit back and let the chips fall where they may. I will wait for the pieces to land and go from there."

"So you're saying you prefer to let circumstances direct your life rather than you being in charge?" I replied, matching his smile. "How about this thought. Making no decision is really making a decision not to decide. It's abdicating responsibility." The group sat quietly, considering the idea.

"One of my favorite lines is, 'I get to choose.' I may not always like my options, I may feel like my choices are limited, I may even be angry that I need to choose. It's important to acknowledge all feelings that go with job transition *and* make choices for moving ahead. So, what's your next step going to be?"

# HOW DO I JUGGLE ALL MY LIVES?

# Drawing the Line

"We live on a lot where our front lawn merges into the next. No fence, no rose bushes, and no line of cedar hedging separate our yard from the neighbor's. And yet when one of our sons pulls out the lawn mower the strangest thing happens. He cuts the grass straight across and then, as if he runs into an invisible wall, he stops, turns the mower around and heads back in front of our home. Why would he do that when the grass extends into the neighbor's yard all the way to their driveway?"

Tyler, often quick to answer, replied, "Because that's your property and your son stopped when he came to the property line."

"But there's nothing there. There's no thick orange paint on the grass. How does he know?" I teased.

"At the back of your yard is likely a stake that shows where your property ends and theirs begins," Tyler explained.

"Exactly, because that's what property lines do for us, isn't it? They define what belongs to me and what doesn't – in another word, ownership. So here's a question for you. What might some of the possible outcomes be if one day my son energetically mowed the whole patch – ours and the neighbors?"

Ellen scoffed and shot me a look of disbelief. "Seriously? Your neighbor would be thrilled to have his lawn cut!"

"I'm not so sure about that," countered Mary. "I grew up beside a man who treated his grass like his baby. He spent hours trimming, watering, fertilizing. If we stepped foot on it he screamed at us. We were terrified to go near it!"

"You've already identified two possible results – a very happy neighbor and a very angry one. What else might happen?" I asked.

"I'd pay the kid!"

"Thanks, Tyler! I'll let my son know. What other outcomes could there be?"

"I suppose your son could be arrested for trespassing, couldn't he?" Mary threw into the discussion.

Ellen looked baffled. "I can't believe this! The kid just mowed someone's lawn. What is wrong with you people?"

"Ellen, let's pursue that idea. This scenario has many possible outcomes, some positive, some negative. Think with me. Is there anything my son could have done to ensure he didn't get thrown in jail?"

Tyler jumped in, "He could have gone to the neighbor first to ask if he'd like his grass cut."

"Yes," I affirmed, "and then my son would be respecting the neighbor's ownership, both parties would have the same expectations and the likelihood of misunderstanding would decrease. What we're really talking about right now is boundaries – what is mine to take care of and what isn't."

"If boundaries are about 'taking care of,' then that makes sense to me," added Ellen. "I feel like I'm always taking care of other people's junk!"

> *"The problem is that other people's garbage lands in our yards."*

I nodded in agreement. "The problem is that other people's garbage lands in our yards. We don't ask for the problem, we often feel like we don't deserve the issues and we seldom desire to expend energy on something we didn't cause. Think of it this way… Someone drives by in the middle of the night and throws a bag of fast food garbage on my lawn. Is it my fault?" No, the class shook their heads unanimously.

"It's not my fault but who is going to clean it up?" I posed.

"Well, it's on your property so it's your job."

I teased and whined in response to Tyler, "But I don't want to clean it up. I didn't put it there!" The class smiled as I asked, "So what are my options?"

Tyler crossed his arms and matched my sassy tone, "You don't have to do anything. Just let it rot on your lawn or hope a strong wind blows it onto your neighbor's grass."

"Oh nice, Tyler," Ellen chided. "I'm glad I don't live beside you."

"But doing nothing is a possibility," I interjected. "Unfortunately, there could be undesirable consequences attached to that such as rodents or others thinking you're a dump site and adding to the garbage. What other choices do you have?"

"I would likely sit in my chair in the living room and fume about the jerk who thinks he can throw his trash on my yard. I would stare at the bag and then will the culprit to come back and pick it up and apologize for putting it there in the first place!" Mary seemed scarily serious.

"And has that worked for you in the past?" I gently questioned.

Mary looked down. "Not the best. I spend a lot of time being angry and alone and waiting for someone else to fix the problem."

Ellen looked over at Mary empathetically. "And the crazy-making thing is, I use all that energy being angry and the bag of junk is still on my property. It doesn't change anything!"

"Boundaries are our protection system. They warn us when something needs attention or cleaning up and they help me define what my responsibility is, and what it isn't. And when life dumps garbage in our yard, part of healthy 'clean up' is to acknowledge and deal with the emotions we feel. What we need to be careful with is not getting stuck in a place of 'poor me' or blaming."

I looked around the room and met with Ellen's confused look and question. "So what do I do – put a sign on my lawn that says 'No Dumping Allowed?'"

I smiled, "Actually, yes, in a manner of speaking, that's exactly what we need to do. Another way to say it is that we need to communicate our boundaries – use words and actions to define where my responsibility ends and yours begins."

Ellen remained puzzled as she posed another question. "I get how a fence is a boundary but communicating my boundaries? How does that work?"

"Our most basic boundary is our skin and it does a few things for us, including keeping the good in – like blood, kidneys, that kind of stuff – and keeping the bad out – like dirt and foreign objects. If you think of emotional boundaries in the same light, we make decisions about how to live based on protecting the good within and keeping harmful things away," I explained.

"Like Mary's grumpy neighbor, you mean?" probed Ellen.

"It definitely includes people. And boundaries can also help us make small, day-to-day decisions that keep us healthy. Let's say my co-worker – we'll call him Bob – asks me for a ride to work one day. It's almost on my way, I know his car is currently broken down, and he's a nice guy so I say yes. A month later, I'm still picking him up each morning and now I'm waiting an extra 30 minutes after I'm done work so I can give him a ride home. He hasn't offered any gas money and regularly tells me his financial woes, which is why he hasn't fixed his car. I feel badly for him but I'm also getting tired of leaving home early and getting home later every day."

Tyler jumped all over that scenario. "The guy is taking advantage of you. He's a free loader!"

"Let's look at this one piece at a time. Whose issue is this?" I asked the group. "Is it Bob's or is it mine?"

The class voted in unison that it was Bob's issue…except for Mary. "I think it's your issue." Her group-mates turned to her, questioning her logic. "Well," she continued, "if you don't want to give him a ride, don't. It's not his fault if you can't say no."

"Let's explore Mary's idea a bit. If I simply sit back and blame Bob for my unhappiness, I am not taking responsibility for my life. I get to choose, and in this case the two most obvious choices are continuing to drive Bob or endure the discomfort of telling him I won't."

"Those are terrible choices," Ellen bemoaned. "I wish people wouldn't ask me in the first place. I hate saying no but I don't like being trapped and driving people to work for the rest of my life either!"

"That feels like it would make things a lot easier, doesn't it? If this was a conversation with any of my sons he would look at me and say, 'I know Mom, life isn't fair!'" The class laughed, recognizing how many times I must have used that line with my children.

"There are other options like negotiating a monthly gas contribution, agreeing to only a morning pick up, putting an end date on the arrangement, that kind of thing. But any of those options would require an honest conversation where I tell him I'm unhappy with the current situation." I continued, "In their book *Boundaries*, authors Cloud and Townsend offer two questions that can clarify situations for us.[4] The first one: 'Is this something the other person ought to do for themselves?' Let's apply this question to Bob. What do you think?"

The class agreed that in the first couple of days it seemed reasonable for Bob to ask for rides because he was in a crisis. When it became a chronic and expected help, maybe it was time to let him sort out a different answer. This idea resonated less enthusiastically with Ellen as she winced again at having to say no to Bob.

"It's true," I affirmed, "these can be uncomfortable exchanges to have. I find it easier when I think that I'm actually not helping Bob if I let him keep taking from me. I'm contributing to his immaturity and perhaps even enabling him. But I don't put my boundary in place to change him – I don't have that power. I put the boundary in place to protect myself."

Ellen shuddered, "Oh, Bob is not going to be happy. I just know it."

"He may not be, but my job is to accept that and let him sort out the rest. How someone reacts to a boundary you set is most often a reflection of their character or boundary issues, not the line you have drawn. I really like Cloud and Townsend's motto: 'When I say no, you may be mad or sad, but that doesn't make me bad.'"

Mary pressed the issue, "But what if I want to help Bob. What if I think he really is down on his luck and just needs a break in life?"

"Thanks for that, Mary, because it leads us to the second question the *Boundaries* authors suggest we ask. 'Is this something I can freely give, without guilt or obligation?' In other words, when I drop Bob off at night and he says, 'See you in the morning,' what's really going on for me? Do I smile on the outside and say 'sure' while on the inside I'm having a conversation of resentment and complaining – you know the one: 'I can't believe he expects me to just show up and drive him every day. I'm so sick of getting home late every night. I could have supper made by the time he finally shows up at the car' and so on. But on the outside, all Bob hears is 'See you tomorrow.'"

"Oh wow. I do that all the time. And that's a boundary issue? Oh dear," Ellen commented.

Tyler came to life. "It may be a boundary issue but it also sounds like an honesty issue to me. If you are saying 'sure' but not wanting to do it at all, isn't that like lying to poor old Bob?"

*"I became aware that every time I said 'yes' with my lips and internally screamed 'no,' I lied."*

"You know, Tyler, that's one of the key realizations that has kept me persisting in developing healthier boundaries," I confessed. "I became aware that every time I said 'yes' with my lips and internally screamed 'no,' I lied. That is inconsistent with my core values and I decided I wanted to live differently."

A collective acknowledgement ran through the room as I continued. "In a perfect world we wouldn't have to deal with things like this. However Bob is a good example of the ways in which boundaries play into everyday life. I may not like having an uncomfortable conversation in order to take care of myself, but it sure beats driving Bob to work for the next ten years!"

# Rocks, Pebbles and Sand

"Today we're talking about time management, or in other words, how to decide what will fill our days. Let's start with this question. When you crawl into bed at night, how do you usually feel about your day?"

"Crawl into bed?" questioned Jill. "I fall into bed! And then I lie there thinking about the things I didn't get done and how much I have to do the next day. There aren't enough hours in the day for me!"

Jake agreed. "I'm pretty sure I could fill 30-hour days and still end up wishing for more time. Between work demands and family responsibilities, I never have time to do the things I really want to do."

"Good point, Jake. And yet there are some people who think twenty-four hours is more than enough time to meet responsibilities, do what's important, and have time to spare. How would you explain that?"

I hardly asked the question before Jake responded, "Seriously? I'd like to know who these people are. I've never met them."

The class echoed similar sentiments, so I confessed, "Well, I guess you have met one now. I can honestly say that's mostly how I feel about my use of time."

Jill spoke up, "Well, you're supposed to. You teach time management!" The class laughed.

"You would hope that follows but I haven't always been able to say this. For years I lived the rat race and then I hit a health crisis and was forced to re-evaluate. I also heard about a study done among people who lived to be ninety or older. When asked if they could live their lives over again, three answers emerged for how they would live differently. Any idea what they said?"

Jenny guessed, "I bet they said something about spending more time with family."

"Yes," I replied, "and specifically with people younger than themselves to be a mentor and help the next generations live well. What else?"

Jake looked reluctant, rolling his eyes as he spoke out. "Oh, they probably wished they had worked less or something like that."

"Close. Consistently these people said they would take more time along the journey to stop and reflect. In hindsight, they attached high value on contemplating and taking in the process, not just measuring progress. That's two. What do you think the third insight might be?"

The group sat quietly.

"Are you reflecting?" I teased. "The last one is risk. People said they would take more chances; try more things, step out of their comfort zone more. Three R's – relate, reflect and risk. So when I get to be ninety I don't want a fourth R – regret. That decision marked significant changes in my life. I don't want to climb into bed any night with regret over how I used my time that day."

Jill looked eager and exhausted. "Okay, I'm ready to hear the secret for how to live like that. I'm sick and tired of feeling like I'm missing the mark. At the rate I'm going, I'll be leading the Regret Club at the senior's home!"

*"I don't want to climb into bed any night with regret over how I used my time that day."*

"Let me tell you about a time in my family life that helped clarify this issue of how to use my time and really how to go about living."

"When our boys were elementary school aged some friends who live among a primitive tribe in Indonesia came for a visit and shared stories of jungle adventures. The tales mesmerized. 'When can we visit them, Mom?' asked our oldest, eyes brimming with desire to swing on vines and swim in piranha-infested waters. 'Someday,' I responded, cringing at the inadequacy of my answer and fully aware the topic was not dead.

Several days later over dinner Taylor repeated his question. I suspected that my attempts to put him off again wouldn't satisfy so I began explaining the cost attached to international travel and the current balance in our savings account – zero. Undaunted he replied, 'Well you guys have always taught us that if something is important enough you make it a priority and work hard to do it. So if we really want to go to Indonesia, that's what we need to do!'"

I addressed the class. "Do you who are parents ever have moments where you wish your kids hadn't been listening to what you were teaching them?" Several class members gave an empathetic nod. "This was one of them and we knew it was time to practice what we preached."

"What followed were several family meetings to determine if we were all on-board and willing to make the sacrifices required to accomplish such a lofty goal. We also discussed what each family member would contribute or give up. Our oldest babysat and had a few odd jobs so he would add his earnings to the fund. The younger two boys had limited earning potential so we brainstormed ideas. Our middle son decided to forego opportunities to snowboard that season and redirected the money to Indonesia travel. The youngest sprang out of his thoughtful silence and offered, 'Mom and Dad, I'm willing to give up having you come and watch some of my soccer games so that you can work more and earn more money!'"

"Now there's an offer that's hard to refuse!" jested Jake.

"Exactly," I added laughing, "but in his world it was a big sacrifice and he viewed it as an honest contribution to the goal.

So over the next two years we made our trip a priority and used that goal to allocate time and resources. It became a go-to point of discernment and led to conversations that sounded like, 'How do you think that fits with our plan for Indonesia?' And let's be clear, our kids asked us that question as often as we posed it to them! We certainly didn't give up living life in those two years and we learned powerful lessons about having clear priorities to direct the use of our time."

"So what happened?" asked Jake. "How does the story end?"

"After two years of saving we spent thirty-four days traveling, flew seventeen times – including helicopter rides through the Balim River Valley – and experienced village life in the jungles of Papua. It proved to be life-changing for us, particularly in seeing how accomplishing a big dream may be achieved through daily decisions."

"That maybe worked for you but I have no money. I can't do the things I really want to do without money." Jill returned to her lack of finances.

"It is true that many things we hope to do have big price tags. I also wonder if the lack of finances is the 'safe' excuse we use for not venturing out. That was certainly my easy-out with our kids. It only became evident to me that money really wasn't my biggest concern when my son challenged me. What do you think were some of the real reasons I hesitated to take such an amazing trip?"

> *"I also wonder if the lack of finances is the 'safe' excuse we use for not venturing out."*

"Honestly, it sounds terrifying to me to go to a jungle. I'd be afraid of being eaten by head hunters or that my kids would be bitten by deadly snakes. So, maybe you were afraid too?" posed Jenny.

I observed several raised eyebrows as I added, "It's true, although the head hunters from that area rarely eat people anymore! But I digress. Jenny is right, fear of many things like failure, the unknown, change, or even success can keep us from stepping out and taking risks. What else do you think played into my uncertainty?"

Jake volunteered, "It just sounds like a lot of work to me. And two years? That's a long time to wait for the payoff."

"Absolutely. Planning to go meant more work, more sacrifices and commitment to stick to the goal for a long time. That's not easy. It required delayed gratification – putting in the effort now for the reward down the road. We live in a culture that's accustomed to instant gratification – 'Why is this computer taking five seconds to find the website? It should go there in one!'"

Jake jumped in, "So you're saying if that's how we expect to live day to day, no wonder it's hard to think of working at something for two years without seeing the rewards."

"Yes…but here's something else I learned through those two years and in all the years since the trip. The actual time in Indonesia was really a small portion of the adventure. The meaningful conversations and opportunities to demonstrate life principles to our sons proved invaluable during the planning and saving stage. But perhaps even less expected is watching these young men live with a vision that is bigger than our little city. Theoretically I knew this was possible. Seeing it is priceless."

My eyes met Jill's and she immediately looked out the window. "Is something about this feeling uncomfortable for you, Jill?" I inquired.

"I think it's great you did that but I don't have any interest in travel and I have no kids to teach. So, how does any of this discussion apply to me?"

"Great question. What is something you would like to see yourself doing a year from now?"

"Well, I've always wanted to own a new car, but I have no money and no job and...."

"Can I interrupt here for a second?"

Jill poked back, "Sure. Are you going to give me a new car?"

"No, but let's explore your desire. What style of car would you like?"

Without hesitation Jill answered, "A red Mazda 323 with a sunroof and awesome sound system."

"Great. Do you have a picture of your dream car?"

Jill shook her head and replied, "No, why torture myself by looking at something I want and can't afford?"

"Or what about this perspective? Every time I go to my fridge or my desk or even my TV, I see a picture of my car and it reminds me of my desired outcome. It keeps the goal fresh and then when I am about to spend money on something impulsively, I might be more inclined to stop and ask if I really need it. Or, would I rather tuck it into my red car account?"

Jill conceded, "Okay that makes sense. But I don't have money to spend impulsively or any way right now."

"Fair enough." I asked the class to join in the brainstorming. "So what are some things Jill can do today or this week that can move her toward her car but don't cost money?"

"She could go to the bank and set up a special account that is only for car savings. That doesn't cost anything to do," offered Jenny to which Jake added, "And she could go to the dealership and find out exactly how much the car costs and maybe even pick up a shiny brochure with a picture or two!"

Jill entered the momentum, "And maybe while I'm at the bank I could ask for some financial advice. I think there are ways I can get rid of some credit cards and do better with managing my money."

"So coming back to our topic of time management and how it applies to your new car, when you get up tomorrow morning, how will your desire for that outcome affect the use of your time?"

Jill considered the question for a moment. "The first thing that comes to mind is that the car idea might actually help me get out of bed. Then I'm thinking that I'll quickly do my around-the-house things so I can go to the dealership – you know, kind of like a reward for doing the boring stuff. I think it could even help me be more motivated to job search because I know that I will need to earn money at some point."

"And that's really what values-based time management is all about. Once we are clear on the things that really matter to us we can use them to determine how our time is best used any given day to make sure we do the important things. Have any of you seen this illustration that Stephen Covey uses?"[5] I pulled out a large clear plastic container and a bucket of fist-sized river rocks. "Here's my version of the illustration."

"Let's call this container my life and fill it up." Two, five, nine rocks in. The eleventh rock reached the rim of the container. "What do you think? Is my life full?"

"Full and then some, I'd say."

I smiled. "Are you sure, Jake? I think there's room for more in my life." I picked up a bucket of gravel and dropped the nickel-sized pieces among the larger rocks. After a few handfuls I grabbed a pail of sand and began pouring it into the airy cracks.

"I see where this is going," Jenny inserted. "The moral of the story is, 'there's always room to do more in life!'" We laughed as I acknowledged, "Oh dear, I certainly hope that's not the only moral. Watch this." I removed five large rocks from the container and the sand collapsed to fill the void. "Jenny, would you please come and put these rocks back in for me?"

> *I removed five large rocks from the container and the sand collapsed to fill the void.*

"Sure, I don't mind getting my hands dirty." Jenny approached the table confidently but struggled to grind the rocks into the sand. After several minutes, and the group offering puzzled looks and chuckles, she set the last two on the table and conceded, "They won't fit. I can't get the sand to move enough to make room for them."

"Thanks for trying. So, I'm curious what the rest of you observed here."

Jill spoke up first. "There wasn't room for the rocks."

"True, yet keep in mind that we didn't add any more rocks and all fit for the initial demonstration. What changed?"

Jarrod broke his quiet observation and noted, "The order changed."

"And Jarrod what applications do you think we can make to my life—to your life— from this illustration?"

"Well," Jarrod paused and thoughtfully considered his response. "I guess we need to pay attention to how we order our lives."

"Yes. If we consider each big rock something we value most, and put them in place first, look how easily other things fit in and around them. But when we fill our days with activities or tasks that don't matter to us, we are hard pressed to find the time for big-rock things that do."

Jake sat forward. "That must be why I feel guilty and frustrated all the time. I'm doing the wrong things first!"

"Now that we have established the starting place for effective time management – clear values – let's take time for each of you to consider what matters most to you."

# I HAVE TO WORK WITH THESE PEOPLE?

# Hooked

It had been a relatively uneventful three weeks with this group. We had arrived at the day on conflict management and I proceeded through the content as usual. I had no idea we would end up where we did as I began with this story.

"Over the years I have spent summer days sitting on the sandy beach of the Fraser River pretending to read my book while my husband fishes for salmon. I say 'pretending' because people-watching fascinates me and I have learned life lessons observing fishers and fish.

Gear matters and starts with a ten-foot fishing pole, a barbless hook and 2-3 ounces of lead weight attached twelve feet from the hook. A fisherman finds firm footing in thigh-deep water and casts his line upstream. The lead ball sinks to the rocky bottom and bounces rhythmically downstream, the line undulating and sweeping the river floor.

Catching sockeye salmon is unlike fishing for trout or other fish. The salmon are on their way up the Fraser River to spawn and die. They are not hungry. They do not strike at bait. So if you catch a salmon it's because the fish has quite literally bumped into your tumbling line while taking in water to breathe. When that happens a skilled fisherman feels the lull from the suspended weight, pulls the rod sharply back, and lodges the hook in the salmon's cheek. 'Fish on!'"

I paused from the story and posed this question. "When the hook is firmly embedded in the fish's mouth, who do you think is in control, the fish or the fisherman?"

The class offered various comments weighing in about equally; half in favor of the fish, half voting for the fisherman. I continued.

"Well, my observation from the riverbank is that it's the fish. I don't mean to give fish too much intellectual credit here, but the one that fights, pulls and tries to swim hard in the opposite direction of the fisherman is often the fish that becomes exhausted with hook further embedded. The patient fisherman keeps the line tight and waits. In other words, the salmon tires itself out, becomes more attached to the fisherman and often becomes dinner.

But what if that fish asks itself, 'Where is the source of my pain?' and then chooses to swim toward the fisherman? As soon as it does, the fisherman will madly reel in the line to keep it taut, but if the fish is fast enough, it usually gets away. Why? The slack line allows the fish to shake its head, spit out the hook, and get free."

The class was quiet and slightly perplexed.

"We're a lot like that fish. We are minding our own business in life and out of the blue we get hooked. We're hurt, offended, wronged and we're angry, sad, resentful and maybe even bitter. If we try to run the other direction or fight hard or seek revenge, we, like the salmon, find our hurt more rooted in us and we remain hooked to the cause of the pain.

But what if we respond like the other salmon? What if we acknowledge the source of our pain and forgive him or her? By identifying the places I'm hooked and choosing to forgive, I allow the hook to fall out which takes away the power of the offender to control me. They can pull and jerk on the fishing rod all they want but the connection to me is gone and I'm free."

As I finished that sentence, Wayne shifted his weight from side to side and shoved his hands repeatedly through his hair, his breathing increasingly audible.

"Don't get me wrong, forgiveness isn't magic. One act of the will to forgive doesn't end the journey, but it can begin a new healing process. The emotional work of forgiveness takes time. It often happens like layers being stripped away and comes in response to other things that happen in life."

Wayne had been relatively quiet and uninvolved for the first three weeks. But now redness shot up his neck to his forehead, and he threw his chair back smashing it against the wall. He swiped up his jacket, jammed his gear under his arm, flung the classroom door open and disappeared with a final slam of the outer door. One client exhaled slowly. Someone else swallowed hard. I reminded myself that I was the teacher.

"Well it seems that story pushed a button for Wayne. How are you all doing, both in response to the story and what just happened?" Careful to respect our angry client and truly never expecting to see him again, I wound the group through a time of debrief and discussion. I dismissed the class and processed the event with my team.

I worked hard to hold back a gasp the next morning when I found Wayne sitting quietly in his usual spot. "Can I say something?" he asked. It's these moments as a facilitator where I find my mind most unhelpful as it races through a realm of possible responses. *Are you kidding me, after yesterday's display!* No, not appropriate. *Will you be throwing furniture this time?* Definitely not. Instead, over pounding heart and held breath I heard myself say, "Of course."

"Your story about forgiveness made me furious, but I guess you all knew that already."

Megan nodded vigorously with wide eyes. Wayne explained how he had gone home and stormed around his empty house shouting: "How dare she tell me to forgive! Who does she think she is? She wasn't the one fired and then screwed around with court battles and four years of misery. I've got three huge binders to prove it! Forgive them? Never!!!" Our collective blood pressure rose as we watched his intensity grow.

Then Wayne became quiet, still and looked directly at me. "And then, in the middle of my rant, something new crossed my mind. I realized that *they* are all fine. It was business as usual at the company. They have gone on with their work and I was being eaten alive by all the hate in me. I knew what I had to do. I went and got my binders. I built a roaring fire, and, one

> "They have gone on with their work and I was being eaten alive by all the hate in me."

page at a time, I burned everything from the court case. All of it. Gone. I had held onto those binders and flipped through those pages over and over for four years. Now they are ashes."

Wayne glanced around the room and offered, "I don't understand it but I feel better. I feel like I'm ready to start living my life again. It doesn't really make sense to me but I know something has changed. I have changed."

We saw many other participants like Wayne who realized that while forgiveness is not a magic pill that will undo injurious circumstances, it can mark a new beginning to get unhooked from past hurts. Emotional healing and moving beyond bitterness and resentment is possible.

# Lunch Anyone?

Bob was a quiet participant, although not unfriendly. He spoke when spoken to and three weeks into the session with his group had developed rapport with his fellow classmates. Perhaps his behavior to this point made his actions so surprising.

I posed a scenario in an attempt to demonstrate how quickly conflict arises over the smallest things. "Let's imagine that my boss is feeling particularly generous today. He walks through this door and says, 'I want to take you all out for lunch in twenty minutes. You decide together and let me know where you want to go' and then he leaves. So class, where would you like to go for lunch today?"

Francis began. "Well, I would like to go to White Spot."

"Thank you. And Mark, how about you?"

"I don't have to pay?" he queried. I shook my head, no. "Okay, then I want steak at the Keg." The group members chuckled at his expensive taste.

Around the room we went: "Thai please", "Red Robin's", "Lou's Grill", "anywhere with good sushi", which led us to Bob, sitting in the back left corner of the room.

"Bob, where would you like to go for lunch?" With no eye contact and arms crossed tightly he snarled, "I'm not going for lunch with you guys!"

I managed to get out "Oh, okay," and continued polling the last three people as the air iced over and people now had arms crossed, eyes narrowed, and faces frowned.

Asking this question in the past typically yielded lighthearted banter and a good discussion about differences of opinion. We would explore how restaurant choice is really a want, not a must-have survival need, and conclude that preferences ought to be held lightly. People often owned treating "wants" like "needs" and routinely we touched on how it could feel safer to conflict over a non-essential than genuinely admit a need. I recall one client who confessed to consistently battling with her spouse over which way the toilet paper came off the roll. As we explored the issue it became apparent that her world felt chaotic and she un-empowered. When the tissue paper came over the top she felt a sliver of control. But admitting her genuine need for control was too vulnerable. Another client summed up the preference issue once as "that's just not a hill I'm prepared to die on." Up to this day our talk involved past experiences and reflections. Never had the fictional "lunch out" scenario created such tension and here it sat, ripe for analysis, on conflict management day.

*"That's just not a hill I'm prepared to die on."*

I considered my options. I could just move on, act as if a client's snub of a free lunch happens all the time and avoid the mess. But I reminded myself that I was the teacher and this could be a great opportunity to model learning. Wow, did the group ever look unimpressed and intimidating though. Yikes.

I inhaled deeply, said a quick prayer and turned to our non-participant.

"Bob," I began gently, "I'm wondering if you would be willing to tell us what would keep you from going out for lunch with us?"

Bob sat back and rolled his eyes. "Phfftd," his only comment. I watched the class watch him and grow in agitation. Their faces screamed, *You anti-social jerk. What have we ever done to you?...* or worse. I envisioned cat-like hissing right around the corner. Things were not improving.

I looked at Bob and repeated my question. "Fine," he muttered. Classmates sat forward, claws poised as I willed myself to breathe.

"I am deathly allergic to five things so I never eat out and never eat food someone else cooked. It could kill me." Bob's explanation hung in the air as he dropped his gaze and curled into himself on his chair. The group waited for me to make the awkward silence go away.

"Thank you for letting us know that, Bob. It's helpful." I paused and looked around at the mix of expressions – guilt, compassion, irritation, confusion. "Would anyone like to comment on what you observed about yourself in this exchange?" More quiet. I waited. Francis eventually spoke up. "I feel really badly at how quickly I jumped to conclusions about Bob. I was so hurt that he wouldn't come with us and kept thinking, 'What's your problem? What have we done to deserve this?' It felt personal to me."

Client after client echoed the sentiment and apologized for judging so quickly, even if they hadn't spoken it out loud. I pushed further. "So what changed the direction of this conflict?"

Mark replied, "You asked Bob what was up."

"I did. One clarifying question started the process of understanding someone else's world and gave you different information to work with."

Jeff spoke honestly. "I admit that I was wrong to jump to conclusions about you, Bob. But man, I gotta tell you, you really made it easy for me to do that. You looked so angry and the way you said it – that you weren't going with US – it was easy to get mad at you. Why didn't you just tell us right away what the deal was?"

*"One clarifying question started the process of understanding someone else's world."*

Classmates turned to Bob with renewed self-righteousness. The angry cats returned.

"I know," Bob replied, "I do that on purpose. In the past, when I've tried to tell people about my allergies they've called me a wimp. They've told me it's all in my head. They've accused me of just being anti-social. I'm sick of it. It's just easier to build a wall and keep people out. It hurts less."

Francis responded, "So you knew you'd put us off and you spoke like that on purpose?"

"Yeah, I guess I did." Bob admitted.

Jeff protested, "Come on, man. Give yourself a break. We aren't all jerks and you don't need to make yourself look like one either."

Bob shrugged, a few others commented, and we proceeded with the remainder of the lesson. But it wasn't business as usual after that discussion for the class or for me. Jeff summed up the participant's experience with, "I guess the moral of the story is not to judge someone before you know their deal." We agreed that maybe, just possibly, one question could begin a dialogue for hearing the experience of the other, decreasing the likelihood of conflict and increasing understanding. I learned afresh to practice what I preach.

And for this particular group that rode the roller coaster of agitation to acceptance, revolt to compassion, ignorance to empathy – all within minutes – there was a happy ending, but not a free lunch out. Instead we celebrated the month by eating potluck together with a menu free of eggs, shrimp, wheat, nuts and soy.

# Belligerent

My first days with the new clients proceeded unremarkably. People offered safe insights about themselves as we navigated early stages of group development and covered course content. At the end of my second day I let the class know that my co-worker, Ann, would take over for four days and then I'd return for another module. Ann and I met, as we did in teaching handoffs, to discuss any classroom concerns. I gave her the basic overview with no red flags and expected a smooth transition.

By the 10:30 break on her first day Ann came into the staff room shaking her head. Amy, our office administrator asked what had happened. Ann responded, "There is one woman, Kerry, who has challenged me at every turn. She is acting like I've offended her and I've only just met her. Maybe she's just having a bad morning."

But the bad morning turned into four days of arguing with Ann, resisting involvement in activities, muttering lewd remarks under her breath, talking to the person beside her during teaching and so on. Ann attempted to check in with Kerry several times to see if the tension could be addressed.

Kerry denied any issue while Ann left each session baffled and frustrated.

"This woman seems bent on sabotaging anything I say or do, and I can't figure out why," Ann shared with our team. "I have no recollection of doing anything to upset her but she absolutely will not engage or cooperate with me. I don't think it's an overstatement to say she is hostile toward me."

Attempts to talk privately with Kerry failed as she refused to meet with Ann. Group tension rose over strained interactions between them. Ann pushed through to the end of her module and handed the class back over to me with relief.

> *"This woman seems bent on sabotaging anything I say or do, and I can't figure out why."*

"Oh good, it's you!" Kerry announced as I stepped into the classroom the next day. The other participants exchanged wary and weary looks. I didn't need Ann's insights or years of teaching to understand this group. I smelled uprising.

"I am glad to be back with you and we will be moving on to a new topic today. Before we do, I know there has been friction and I'd like to address that first."

Kerry needed no further invitation. "The problem was that other instructor. Now that she's gone, we'll be fine."

"Seriously?" interjected Allan. "You don't think you had anything to do with what happened in here?"

"No. It was her fault. I didn't do anything wrong."

"Seriously?" repeated Allan. "You don't think you were uncooperative and difficult? You didn't do one thing she asked us to do! Unbelievable!"

Joy picked up on Allan's rant. "I agree with Allan. Kerry, you made the last few days miserable for all of us. You couldn't just let something be, you had to argue every step of the way."

Others in the class looked poised to jump into the fray so I stood up and moved into the center of the U-shaped table. "Let's pause and take a breath. Just like in work places you are being asked to work together with people who are potentially very different than you. So, let's see if we can sort this out."

One participant sighed while another shot me a "you're nuts" look. I began again. "Kerry, I'm hearing reports that others felt you weren't willing to fully participate in these last few days." Allan snorted as I continued. "Can you tell me what's been going on for you?"

"Nothing's going on," she insisted.

"So how do you explain the comments from your fellow classmates about you not participating and even arguing with Ann?"

Kerry paused and stared at me. "Well, maybe I didn't do everything she asked. But I don't have to."

"You certainly are free not to participate. I'm just curious what kept you from entering in."

Again, Kerry stared hard at me before she spoke. "Maybe I just don't like her. Maybe she doesn't deserve to have me do what she says." Kerry's jaw tightened and her volume increased. "I knew the minute she walked through that door on the first day that I would not give her the satisfaction of doing anything she asked." Kerry slammed her hand down on the table as she finished.

I stood still surveying the expressions of shock and disbelief among the other clients. "So you made a choice to not join in early on. Can you tell me what that's about?"

"I just did!" Kerry shot back and through gritted teeth replied, "She doesn't deserve my respect!"

"I see. Did she do or say something to offend you?"

Without pause Kerry spit back, "She didn't have to. She looks exactly like my teacher in grade four who told me I was stupid and that I would never amount to anything. There was no way I was going to let that happen again! So I shut her down before she had a chance!" Kerry sat back in her chair with an air of accomplishment.

Allan broke the silence. "Seriously? She's not *actually* your teacher. Why are you punishing her for what someone else did forty years ago?"

Kerry cocked her head and put on a "seriously" look of her own. "I told you. She deserved it."

I entered in. "Well, the teacher who said those hurtful things to you years ago is the one in question. It was wrong of her to speak to you that way. And Kerry, Allan is right. Ann is not that teacher. And even if she looks just like her, she's not the same person. Do you see that?"

Kerry responded defensively, "I don't care. No one is going to hurt me like that again. I'm not taking the chance."

"Our past hurts can affect our choices. Let me explain what I think is going on here from a brain science perspective. When we're young we store all kinds of messages in the amygdala or what some have called the emotional brain. That's the part connected to our survival instinct. Have you heard of the fight or flight response?"

"Yes," replied Joy, "that's what kicks in when we're in danger, right?"

"That's it, yes. The emotional part of our brain is designed to be reactive in order to save our lives. Unfortunately that reactive portion doesn't have the capacity to distinguish between physical and emotional threats. So when something in the present triggers an emotional wound from the past our brain goes into a reactive mode and our first response is not rational thinking. In fact we often become so flooded with the chemicals generated for fight or flight that we behave as if we're in danger of dying. The feeling can be intense – and irrational – unless we learn to identify what's happening and engage a different part of our brain – the prefrontal cortex. That's the thinking part. If we can engage it we can talk ourselves off the ledge."

"What do you mean by that?" Joy inquired.

"Let me give you a personal example. As a child I presented as independent and precocious but I really had a sensitive nature. So when my parents had lots of people over for loud parties that went late into the night I often felt scared and lonely. I would hide in my bedroom and talk to my friend Raggedy Ann. Each night I would look at the little red heart on her chest that said 'I love you' and find comfort.

Fast forward forty years with the doll lost and long forgotten and I'm in an antique store with a friend. I walked past this cradle and a Raggedy Ann doll caught my eye. I smiled and kept walking a few steps but something drew me back. Before I could think about it, I picked her up and stared at the heart on her chest. My friend looked over to see me sobbing right in the middle of the store!"

"So what do you think happened for me?" I asked the group.

Joy replied, "Well, first thing, where are the Kleenex? That story breaks me up." She wiped her eyes, blew her nose and continued. "I guess the doll reminded you of being that scared little girl."

I nodded. "I think so. The rush of emotion was incredible. But here's the point of it all. I wasn't that five-year-old anymore. I could feel raw emotion ambush me *and* I could step back and consider it from my adult perspective. I didn't have to be held hostage by my childhood hurt and emotions."

Kerry sat forward and glared at me. "That's not what I'm doing!"

"Would you be willing to give the idea some consideration?"

Without thought Kerry replied, "I don't need to. It's not me."

*"'Does this response fit the situation?' and if not, then I have a meeting with myself and try to determine what's really happening for me."*

"Well I am learning that when I feel a huge emotional reaction to something it's helpful to ask myself this: 'Does this response fit the situation?' and if not, then I have a meeting with myself and try to determine what's really happening for me."

Allan laughed out loud. "I like that phrase – 'have a meeting with myself!' I'm going to try that."

"It has helped me sort out where my responses and feelings are coming from to ask a few simple questions like: 'What's really going on here?' or 'What am I afraid of?' It can even be: 'Do I need a time-out?' It's asking myself whatever I need to determine the root of the emotional reaction."

"Is that even possible?" questioned Joy.

"Not always and not likely fully. But it has helped me discover clues about what's happening for me and it's given me a stronger ability to live in the present."

Allan inquired, "What do you mean by living in the present?"

"We all live from our past in the present because we are an accumulation of experiences, hurts, successes, etc. The past creates a lens through which we see the present. So, let's go back to Raggedy Ann for a moment. Did that doll in that cradle in that antique store do anything to cause me to cry?"

"No, it didn't seem like it," Allan observed.

"Right, but she triggered something in my brain from the past and in that present moment emotion surfaced. It wasn't the doll's fault but if I don't understand how this works, I just feel the emotional reaction and end up saying, 'Stupid doll! Quit making me cry!'"

Joy smiled, "No wonder we say and do things that look ridiculous and don't seem to make sense. But what I really want to know is what did you do that day in the store?"

I grinned. "I did what all forty-five-year-old women crying in antique stores do…I bought the doll!"

Everyone applauded my decision, except Kerry. "This is ridiculous. Are we going to just sit here and talk about this all day?"

"I think we are ready to move on to our topic now unless there are other questions or comments."

Over the next several days Kerry remained distant and largely uninvolved. She rarely participated and yet her attendance remained perfect, arriving early each day and staying to the end. When the class finished she brought food for the celebratory potluck the last day but remained silent as each person shared what the class had meant to them. We fully expected her goodbye to be permanent.

About three months later we received a call from Kerry informing us that her new job required her to do some hiring. "I like what you do over there and am wondering if you can recommend to me anyone who has come through your program."

I like to think this was Kerry's way of acknowledging that something in her time with us made a difference in her life, but then again, maybe she just wanted an employee.

# WHERE IS THE "I" IN TEAM?

## To The Moon

"No, that's not what we're supposed to do," clarified Ed. "We're just supposed to rank them in order of their importance to us." Valerie snapped, "I don't really care. I'm not walking 200 miles!"

And so began the team-building exercise called *The Moon Problem*. I had divided the class into three groups of four, and two teams settled quickly into the task of assessing the fifteen items which survived the crash-landing of a space craft on the moon. Survival meant walking 200 miles from the accident site to the space station. The astronauts – each class group – needed to agree on the importance of the items in helping achieve their goal. The most critical articles received rankings one, two, three and least valuable were to be labeled thirteen, fourteen, and fifteen.

"Okay," Ed tried again, "how about we each read over the instructions and items to ourselves and then we'll talk about it."

"No. I already told you. I'm not walking 200 miles so I don't need to read anything." Valerie retorted.

In fairness to these "astronauts" this activity had a reputation for evoking diverse responses from participants. Typically I would observe group interactions from a distance, watching for communication styles with hope that the previous day's topic of healthy conflict management would be evident. Occasionally I would drop in and ask a question or two, or perhaps offer some clarification, but I worked hard at not being too involved.

> *Experience taught me that some of the best learning came when the going got rough.*

Experience taught me that some of the best learning came when the going got rough– like the teams these people could work on some day. I usually took about half an hour after the exercise to debrief it and coach the group through self-discovery and personal application.

Not so this day.

Jackie, the third member of Ed and Valerie's group, made a suggestion. "Why don't we each rank the items privately and then compare?"

"There's no point. I want a buggy of some sort, and until we agree to that I'm not doing anything," Valerie declared.

"We're not supposed to build a buggy!" Ed insisted.

Martin, the remaining member, tried to calm the others. "Look, if we just take a breath and step back from this…"

Ed jumped in, "Exactly, take a breath, and if we don't rank oxygen as number one, there won't be any breathing going on! We'll all be dead."

Jackie agreed. "So let's put it as number one then and since there's no oxygen on the moon let's put matches as fifteen because they won't work without oxygen."

"No way!" Valerie's volume increased. "The only power source we have is to light the oxygen and shoot our buggy across to the space station. I'm not putting matches at fifteen!"

Valerie's teammates looked astounded. Around and around they went, Jackie trying to reason, Martin attempting to find compromise and Ed repeating the rules over and over. Eventually Ed threw down his pen and conceded, "You know what. Have it your way. I'm done."

Jackie and Martin looked at each other and acknowledged defeat, weary from Valerie's adamant protesting and continual no-walking resolve. The group lost its vision for the goal as Valerie repeatedly argued her position. In all my years observing this game I would have to give Valerie the prize for relentless pursuit of a personal agenda.

And her group paid the price. I proceeded with the scoring process and I'm pretty sure it would be mathematically impossible to get a sorrier result than the one Valerie's group achieved. Certainly they set the worst-ever record for my classes. To say her fellow team members were displeased would make mockery of what ensued.

This relatively reserved bunch that had plodded through and eventually acquiesced to each of Valerie's demands lost it. Like an erupting volcano, accusations, blame and name calling spewed from all three. I jumped off my chair, hand raised in "stop" mode and moved directly into their space. "Whoa!" I blurted to stem the lava flow. I caught looks of distress from other groups and could only imagine what they were thinking. I knew what my 'inside voice' screamed. *Seriously people? You aren't even really on the moon! But right now, I sure wish you were! Filters, Shelaine, filters.*

# CHANGING COURSE

"You are the most self-centered person I have ever worked with!" Ed charged. "This was supposed to be a team exercise and all you could think about was yourself and that stupid buggy idea."

"You arrogant son of a..." Valerie began to counter.

"Hold on," I interrupted. "Let's slow this down a bit. I think we should take a break. We will come back in ten minutes and sort our way through this. Grab a coffee, get a breath of fresh air and move around. And please, save your comments about this exercise for when we reconvene – just take a break for now."

> *"You are the most self-centered person I have ever worked with!"*

The group dispersed and I dove into the staff room and shut the door. I needed the break to brainstorm with my co-workers. "You would not believe what just happened!" I began. My team bantered helpful ideas with me but the ten minutes went by far too quickly.

Over the next three hours – not the typical thirty minutes – we debriefed the exercise. What began as ugly, venomous attacks settled into angry exchanges which worked their way down to simmering discussion and me seriously considering asking for a pay raise. I pressed on.

I tried approaching Valerie from yet another angle. "How would you say your approach to this task affected your group?"

"My approach? They were just a bunch of..."

"Hold on, Valerie. I've listened to your frustrations about your group and heard their perspective as well. We've covered that ground. Now I'm asking you to think about your role in the breakdown of your team. So let me ask you again, how did your approach to the task affect your group?" My insides quaked as my "outside voice" challenged her.

She leaned toward me prepared to strike and then paused, catching herself, sitting back and becoming silent. "I can be a bitch and I like to have things my way."

"Thank you for that, Valerie. And so is there anything you'd like to say to your group?"

"I still think we shouldn't have to walk 200 miles," she began. *Oh, help* ran through my mind as I watched Ed, Martin and Jackie roll their eyes. But she conceded, "I guess there might have been some other ways to do it."

As much as I would love to have heard a more forthright apology for her obstinate behavior I dared not push her further on the issue. I felt exhausted but more work remained.

"And how about the rest of you in the group – what can each of you see as your part in the conflict?"

Silence. The three stared at me. Finally, Ed spoke. "Well, I think we needed more backbone. If we were really on the moon we would have all died and I don't think that was necessary. At some point we should have given Valerie an ultimatum to get on board and if she didn't we should have cut off her oxygen supply."

Valerie burst out laughing and, much to everyone's surprise, added, "Yeah, I guess I deserved that."

Wow.

I opened the next question up to the whole class. "So in terms of working with teams here on earth, what do you think 'cutting off one's oxygen supply' could look like?"

Mike offered, "In the biggest sense, it could mean someone is fired from the company or at least that project or team."

Kathy added, "I think it's about the team members not being run over and then playing dead. I mean, not believing they were powerless and had to give in."

"It's true that in team there is a two-way responsibility. A healthy group will provide a safe atmosphere where we can share our opinions and expect to be heard. Group members don't have to agree but the goal is to disagree respectfully. The other side is in the way we share our ideas with the group. We are only one member and must work at keeping our agenda and needs in balance with the larger goals and purpose of the team." I added.

*"So we pretty much demonstrated how not to be a team, didn't we?"*

Martin interjected, "So we pretty much demonstrated how not to be a team, didn't we?"

"In light of what I just said, I suppose so. But, look at where you are now. Teams will hit rough patches and sometimes come to an impasse. What's important then is what you do about it. Today you had ready access to me as facilitator, but in a work situation you may have to take the initiative to call someone in to help – like a supervisor or other team leader or perhaps an outside consultant. It's not *that* you encounter issues; it's *how* you address them. Teams without conflict stagnate and lose their creativity and edge."

"What?" questioned Jackie. "Say that last part again. About conflict."

I repeated the phrase and expanded, "What I mean is that conflict in a team can challenge us to make sure we are on the right track, not just going with the old ways because they are easy. Conflict can generate new ideas and fresh vision."

"And it can create total meltdowns and stalemates!" Martin added.

"Fair enough," I conceded. "The key is finding our way through it and not losing sight of why we are on the team in the first place."

I glanced at the clock to see that technically enough time remained to do one more team activity. Instead, I smiled at the weary astronauts and dismissed the group early.

# Building Mania

The three groups of three members each awaited my instructions for the third team-building activity of the day. The interactions so far had been cooperative and playful.

"This next exercise involves building something," I began. "Please decide who will be your team's builder and who will be your two information gatherers."

In an earlier activity we discussed the importance of each person's role in group dynamics. I overheard Manny coaching his group. "We need to match skill with role. Who's good with their hands? Who's better with words?"

"Here's your task. Out front, at the desk, is a Lego model. Your job is to create – in this room – an exact replica of what's out there."

I went on to explain that the builders were the only people who could touch the materials and they could not leave the classroom. In other words, the builders would never see firsthand what they were making and would rely only on the instructions brought to them by their teammates.

The information people could make as many trips to the reception area as they needed, but only one at a time. They could not touch the model or the materials and upon their return could only use words and gestures to convey directions. No cell phone pictures, no drawings, just verbal descriptions.

"Is this a competition?" asked Nora.

"No, and it's not a timed activity either. Take however long you need to finish the task," I clarified. "Any other questions?" The groups looked eager to start. "No? Okay then, here are your building materials." I reached into my box and pulled out three bags of Lego each containing exactly the same number, color and shapes of pieces. As I handed them out I added, "Just to be clear, each bag contains everything you need to build an exact replica of the model out front." I didn't mention that I included one extra, unnecessary piece.

And with that they were off.

Oliver, Team 1's builder, called Manny and Nora in close. "Listen, we need a strategy here. Nora, you go see what we're building. Then we'll decide how to proceed." Manny nodded his agreement and Nora headed out the door.

Builder Fran from Team 2 began sorting the pieces – blue here, red there, wheel and odd parts separated from the rest. She worked in earnest, oblivious to her lingering teammates. Deidre and Ev exchanged "whatever" looks, shrugged their shoulders and decided Deidre would go out first.

Team 3's Patty zipped out and returned quickly to the classroom. "I have no idea what that is! It's not anything! It's not a car or a house or anything I've ever seen before. It's just a bunch of Lego stuck together. I'm not doing this. It's stupid!" She flopped into a chair.

"Okay, I'll go," offered Holly.

Periodically I wandered to the front desk to check with the receptionist and observe the players. Deidre raced down the hall and skidded to the counter in her sock feet. She turned to me and accused, "You've changed it! This is not the same as the last time I came out!"

"Actually, I haven't touched it, have I Amy?" Our receptionist confirmed that I had not altered the model and quickly added that neither had she. Deidre mumbled something about losing her mind and headed back to the classroom.

Manny arrived and spoke through the Lego layers out loud. He looked at me and shook his head. "Seriously. There's got to be some memory-sucking vortex in this hallway. By the time I get back there I draw a total blank."

It took about fifteen minutes for all groups to conclude that they had created an exact copy of the Lego structure. Team 1 appeared to be finished but had hidden their statue behind a binder standing on edge. I decided to leave that question until later in the debriefing.

I brought in the prototype and compared it to each team's work. Two had it correct and one team had incorporated the extra, unnecessary piece. After receiving some general feedback Deidre spoke. "I'm sorry I accused you of changing the statue out there. I thought for sure you were playing with our heads."

"No, I really wasn't."

"I disagree. Or maybe you just lied to us," challenged Ev.

I raised my eyebrows at the suggestion. "How so?"

"You told us we had only what we needed to build this but you put in an extra piece we didn't need. Do you know how many extra trips I made trying to find where that stupid long white piece fit? And then we lost the whole game because we figured it had to go somewhere. You gave it to us!"

Oliver jumped in. "No, Shelaine didn't say we had *only* what we needed. She said we had *everything* we needed, right?" He looked to me to confirm.

"It's true that I said 'everything you need' and I'm glad you bring this up Ev. It sounds like your team made an assumption that you had to use all the pieces."

Ev agreed reluctantly. "Well yeah. Otherwise why would you have given it to us?"

"You were playing with our heads," Deidre laughed.

"I guess you could say that. I prefer to think of it as increasing your opportunity for learning," a comment met with groans. "But seriously," I continued, "assumptions play a significant role in teams and often lead to misunderstandings and unnecessary conflict. The best way to avoid that is to ask clarifying questions. In this case Deidre found out I wasn't changing the statue because she asked me."

*"Assumptions play a significant role in teams and often lead to misunderstandings and unnecessary conflict."*

"Accused you, actually." Deidre threw in. "Thanks for the nice interpretation."

I continued, "So, Ev, what kept you from asking me about the extra piece?"

"I assumed..." she caught herself as she said the word. "Yeah, I guess I assumed we weren't allowed to ask you anything. You would have answered me?"

I nodded and carried on. "Teams get into trouble when they don't ask for help. It's a rare situation where a group has everything they need and requires no outside input. Asking questions of each other and requesting help from beyond the team is important. So, what other assumptions did you make during this exercise?"

"I assumed that we would win!" Oliver declared. "And we did!" His team cheered victoriously until Holly squelched their enthusiasm. "How can you win when it isn't even a competition? Shelaine said it wasn't."

"Augh, call it whatever you like but we finished first and we got it right so I'm pretty sure that makes us the winner!" Oliver leaned back, hands behind his head.

"Oliver, I'm interested to know your intent with the binder wall," I invited.

Oliver's team explained the plan that they had agreed to early on – to bring back details and double check each other's work. The system seemed slow and onerous at first but it soon became clear they were onto something. While the other groups struggled and debated if layers and colors fit correctly, Oliver's team finished and confidently set aside the extra piece.

"And the wall? Why did you hide your creation?"

Oliver replied, "I noticed that Fran used our model to build theirs. She wasn't even listening to her people, just looking over here and copying us. She was cheating, so I hid it."

I felt confident in the rapport I had developed with Oliver and believed he could take a little challenge, so I pushed back.

"Let me see if I have this straight. This wasn't a competition. There was no time limit. You had three teams for this activity but you are all part of this one class team. Minutes before this you worked with members from other teams to survive on the moon. See where I'm going with this?"

"But why should they just get to copy when we did the hard work?" Oliver protested with a smile.

"Or how about this perspective? Imagine your small teams are part of a company. You are the marketing department. You are the accounting group. You are research and development. Each has its mandate but needs information from the others to accomplish the goals of the company."

"Then you should have told us that at the beginning! It's your fault we hid our tower," Oliver jested.

"I agree…sort of. I'm not going to accept blame for the hiding part but I do agree that communicating expectations gives people parameters they need to work." Oliver seemed satisfied with my concession.

"We've heard about one team's strategy. How about the rest of you?"

Deidre spoke up. "I have no idea what you'd call our strategy except frustrating! I'd leave and look at the model and work hard to remember the order. By the time I came back the contraption in the classroom had been changed! Fran would listen to us and then add her own twist. We wasted so much time undoing and redoing."

"I was bored," Fran countered immediately. "You guys couldn't agree on the design so I entertained myself. What's the big deal? We got it right in the end."

"And were last to finish!" Deidre retorted.

I intervened. "Let's go back to your comment about being bored Fran. I attended a session recently on brain science and the presenter said that boredom is really a euphemism for anxiety. That's a new idea to me. Do you guys agree with that? Fran, did you feel anxious during this?"

Fran stared at me. "Well, actually, I guess I did. It was hard for me to be stuck here and not see for myself what I was building. I kept getting different messages – 'put this here, no take it off, put that one there.' I didn't know who to believe so I made it up as I went. And I looked over at Oliver's model because they seemed to know what they were doing."

"So what do you take from this experience?"

"That I'm more controlling than I thought!" Fran laughed self-consciously.

*I stood up and wrote "BRAVING" on the whiteboard.*

"Well, by the number of heads nodding right now I'd say you're not alone. I want to return to something you said a minute ago. It was about not knowing who to believe – an issue of trust perhaps?"

I stood up and wrote BRAVING on the whiteboard – Brene Brown's acronym for the anatomy of trust: Boundaries, Reliability, Accountability, Vault, Integrity, Nonjudgment, Generosity.[6]

"We've talked about boundaries and reliability – doing what you say you'll do is pretty self-explanatory. Brown sees accountability as taking ownership of mistakes, apologizing and making amends. The vault refers to my ability to hold confidences. How can you trust me with your personal experiences if I'm sharing someone else's private information with you?"

"I'd never thought of it that way," Fran offered.

I went on to explain that integrity, as defined by Brown, is choosing to practice your values rather than just professing them. Holding a non-judmental posture allows each person to ask for what they need and the conversation to flow without criticism. Finally, I explained generosity in the context of trust.

"Brene Brown is referring here to generosity of interpretation. In her words, will you 'extend the most generous interpretation possible to the intentions, words, and actions of others?'"

"That's all great but it's pretty hard to trust your teammate when she flat out refuses to do anything!" Holly snarled at Patty. Apparently it was team 3's turn to weigh in.

"Whatever!" Patty retorted. "It was just Lego. I didn't ask to be put on a team. I hate teams."

"So you just quit?" I questioned. Patty nodded defiantly. "It's true this was just about Lego. But the reason I do these activities is to give opportunity to see how you function as team members. Workplaces are full of teams today."

"Well I'm never going to work on a team anyway so it doesn't matter. I'm going to start my own bookkeeping business and work by myself from home." Patty crossed her arms and sat back as if the conversation had ended.

"Fair enough, perhaps team won't be a big part of your future. However you are part of a team today and they aren't very pleased with how it went. Can you see another way you could have handled this?" My blood pressure rose as I waited for Patty. And her team waited. The whole group waited in awkward silence. Nothing.

"While you take some more time to think, let me ask your teammates something. Holly and Ray, what would have made this a better experience for you?"

Ray spoke for the first time. "If Patty could have told us right away that she didn't like teams and didn't want to do this activity that would have been easier. Because she didn't we kept trying to include her and her stubbornness got old quickly."

Holly added, "I agree. We wasted a lot of time and energy coaxing her when we could have just done the work."

I spoke to the class. "Other people can't read our minds so we need to communicate what we're thinking. It lessens misunderstandings and conflict." I turned back to Patty. "So, do you want to add anything now?" I inquired.

"No. Just don't put me on another team."

"Alright. We've got one more activity today and Patty, you are welcome to sit this one out."

# WHERE DO I GO NOW?

# Open Hand, Closed Hand

I stood with my arms extended, one hand in a tightly-held fist and the other palm up. "What does this image convey to you about goals?"

Brett chewed on his lip. "It feels confusing – like you can't decide between two options."

"Thanks, Brett. Anybody else want to comment?"

Zoe, the youngest in the room blurted, "I like your hands because that's how I feel about goals. The open hand says 'bring it on' and the closed fist says 'I can't do this.'"

"Thanks, Zoe." I began to raise my fist higher, "For me this represents the need to hold tightly – even fiercely at times – to my goals. And my open hand reminds me that I need to be willing to change along the way. This openness may even acknowledge that the goal will shift as I move ahead."

Zoe flopped back in her chair. "Okay, if I think of goals like that, I can probably work with them. I've always thought that goals constrain me. I say I'm doing one thing, then something else gets my attention so I go after it. I want it all! Love-hate, like I said before."

"You're moving us in the direction I hoped we'd start with today. What do the rest of you think about goals?"

Brett continued biting his lip. "Goals feel like something I should do, so I feel guilty when I don't. But honestly, I'm terrible at reaching goals. As soon as I feel like I have an idea someone in my life suggests something else and then I'm so conflicted. I want the goal but I don't want to disappoint or upset the people around me. I really don't like this topic at all."

Rita jumped in. "And I couldn't feel more differently. Goals are my life. I wake up in the morning with a mental list and then I do it. At the end of the day I feel satisfied knowing I've accomplished things I care about!"

"I appreciate your honesty and I bet if we went around the room there would be similar thoughts from your peers. Part of what you've just described is related to your personal styles and we're going to talk about that in a few minutes. My guess is your comments are also influenced by past experience with goals. So let's start there."

I explained to the group how we would be approaching goals considering where we've come from, where we are now and where we'd like to go.

"So when you think of your past, how is it likely to hinder you from setting and accomplishing goals today?"

"Like I just said. I have a long history of not following through on what I set out to do. Can't say there's much motivation to keep banging my head on that wall." Brett's shoulders sagged and he slouched forward onto his elbows. "Why even bother?"

"Well Brett that reminds me of a story I heard about a baby elephant in a circus being kept in place by a single chain around its ankle. Initially the elephant would tug and pull but the chain kept it tethered to a stake in the ground. Soon the animal learned that its efforts were unrewarded and it quit trying to break free."

"Poor baby elephant," empathized Zoe.

"Yes it's sad to think of elephants held like that in captivity. What's telling to me though, and related to our topic, is that the gauge of the chain is never increased over the elephant's lifespan. The elephant will grow in size and strength – enough to snap the chain and escape – but it doesn't. Why do you think that is?"

"Because he believes he can't. Oh man, I'm really an elephant at heart!" Brett bemoaned.

"'Because he believes he can't'…exactly. And just like we've explored over these weeks together, we have incorporated incorrect beliefs about ourselves that can keep us chained in inactivity. If that elephant could have a conversation with itself, what might he be saying?"

*"We have incorporated incorrect beliefs about ourselves that can keep us chained in inactivity."*

Zoe kicked into acting mode. "Poor me. Here I am chained to this stake after all these years. I'll never go anywhere, never see the world, never amount to anything. I'm stuck here and there's nothing I can do about it. Boo hoo!"

"Yup," Brett chimed. "I am most definitely an elephant!"

"Brett, here's a question for you. Would you like to leave that elephant mindset behind? Are you willing to challenge your own self-talk and see yourself in a different light?"

He shifted in his chair and avoided eye contact. "Well I think I'm starting to see that I need to. I want to. I'm just not sure I can."

"Keep in mind that change starts with the recognition that it needs to happen and then progresses one step at a time."

"Hey, you mean 'baby steps'...like the guy in *What About Bob*?"

"Exactly, 'baby steps!' And keep in mind that our personal style connects to goals. It might be a comfort to know that you aren't alone in your goals challenges."

We spent the next portion of class time looking at how each style – Behavioral, Cognitive, Interpersonal and Affective – address goal-setting. The discussion concerning Behaviorals was appropriately short and to the point.

"Do you recall what Rita said earlier about goals? I think it could be summarized like this, 'I have them and I do them.'" Rita affirmed the statement and I explained further. "Behaviorals are wired to accomplish tasks so they thrive from a goal-driven model. It comes naturally to them. They think future – where do I want to go – and then present – what do I need to do to get there? Then they do it."

Rita beamed. "That's me."

"How about Cognitives? What do you think their approach is to goals?"

Davi, who scored high in the C category, spoke up. "I don't like being rushed. I think through things, consider my options, research if I need to, and then make a detailed plan."

I nodded. "Once again personal style keeps showing up. Cognitives like order and desire a quality outcome for their goal. So they will put in the time to analyze the past – what worked, what didn't – and look to the future with their systematic approach. So that's Cognitives in a nutshell. How about Interpersonals?"

"Since I'm a high Interpersonal, I'm going out on a limb and guessing that we take the elephant approach." Brett chuckled.

"Well, you may not want to make *that* big a statement, Brett, but something you shared earlier is true of an Interpersonal's wiring. They set goals with others in mind and hope that their goals don't upset relationships. They are often practical goal-setters and don't lean toward big risks like the Behaviorals."

"And what about Affectives? Don't forget about us!" Zoe teased, only half joking.

"Don't worry, Zoe, Affectives are hard to miss! They tend to have open-ended goals so they can flow, flex, and change. A fixed target feels too constraining. What if something better catches your attention, right?"

"Absolutely!" she agreed.

"And Affectives can become frustrated with themselves because they don't follow through; they can end up feeling like they haven't accomplished what others around them have."

"Absolutely!" Zoe shouted again. "But I sure have fun getting nowhere!"

On that note we broke for coffee and agreed that our goal would be to return in fifteen minutes and talk about a time-tested strategy for setting and reaching goals.

# Zig-Zag

"Have any of you heard of Zig Ziglar?" I posed as we continued our discussion of goals.

"You've got to be kidding. That can't be the guy's real name? Is he from back in the day?" asked Kai. She, like other twenty-somethings, was too young to recognize the goal-setting icon who led the motivational world with his 1975 book, *See You at the Top*.[7]

"It actually wasn't his real name. He was born Hilary Hinton but 'Zig Ziglar' has greater intrigue for the man who was once the most sought-after personal development trainer in North America.[8] When I came to work here my boss asked me to teach goal-setting and he gave me a video by Zig Ziglar – and for good reason. The concepts Ziglar presented are ideas still widely used today. We're going to take a look at it in a moment. First, let me tell you one of my favorite Zig-stories.

Jean Henry Fabre, a nineteenth-century French entomologist placed Processionary Caterpillars around a flower pot and observed as they formed a circle following one another around and around, non-stop. After a few days,

Fabre put pine needles (caterpillar food) in the center of the pot and watched in disbelief as they continued circling and after seven days dropped dead from starvation and exhaustion with food only inches away. Ziglar concluded that the insects confused activity with accomplishment.

Ziglar pioneered work in the motivational field and many followers have taken his seven principles and adapted them. You may have heard of setting S.M.A.R.T. goals or related methods. If a different approach works for you, go for it, but how about giving this old-school system a shot?"

I pointed the class to their handouts and we began with Ziglar's first step – *Identify the objective.*

> *"How about giving this old-school system a shot?"*

We discussed the need for an objective to be specific so we know what we are shooting for; to have measurable qualities, allowing us to identify when we have arrived; and be achievable to set ouselves up for success. For example, better to aim for contacting three companies, than to say "I've got to find a job."

"The second step is pretty self-explanatory – *Write down an expected completion date.* Again, make it realistic so you have enough time to accomplish the goal but not so much time you lose motivation. For example, 'I will contact three companies by next Thursday.'"

"I like the third principle – *Identify obstacles.* What hurdles will you encounter as you move toward your target?"

"Me!" Nate threw his hands into the air. "Seriously, I'm my biggest obstacle. I procrastinate. I get distracted. I change my mind. I'm the only one to blame for not meeting my goals."

"For me it's money," added Kai. "I want to go to school but education costs a lot and I'm broke."

"So for now write down those things and let's look at the fourth point – *Name people and/or organizations you'll need help from*. This may be counselors, student loans officers, family, friends – anyone who can help you move ahead. What you don't want are people like the characters in this next story.

I heard about an experiment where five monkeys were placed in a room. In the center stood a pole loaded with ripe bananas at the top. The monkeys all spied the feast and headed straight for it. However, the researchers shot water and soaked every monkey who grabbed for the bananas. Each attempt resulted in an icy shower and after a few douses the band of monkeys sat in the corner angry and dejected."

"Hey, I think I know those monkeys!" kidded Nate.

"Maybe you do! At this point, the researchers sent in a new monkey oblivious to the history of the five. I think monkey number six took a look at his peers and thought, 'What's your problem? There are perfectly good bananas right there and I'm going to have them. Your loss!' What do you think happened next?"

Lisa speculated, "I'd put money on the new monkey getting doused like the rest of them."

"That's what I thought when I first heard this. But interestingly, that's not what happened. Before the newcomer could get any distance up the pole the five monkeys jumped up, grabbed his legs and pulled him down."

"Wow, nice friends. They kept him from being drenched," Lisa observed.

"Fair enough. And what about this other perspective? What if the researchers had no intention of watering the new monkey? What if he actually could have had the bananas but his beaten down 'friends' kept him from trying?"

*"So, are you saying we're the bunch of monkeys?"*

Nate scratched his rib cage on both sides and asked "So, are you saying we're the bunch of monkeys?"

"I'm not touching that comment!" I teased. "But I am wondering what kind of support group you have. Are you surrounded by people who cheer you on, encourage you to risk, and stand behind you when you venture out? Or do you have a collection of 'dripping monkeys' who would rather hold you back from achieving your goals?"

Lisa protested, "But I still think maybe they were being nice and trying to protect their friend."

"I agree that healthy friends will speak into our lives if they see us taking unnecessary or unhealthy risks and, if we're wise, we'll listen to their counsel. I also know that sometimes people get stuck in their own hurt and disappointment and want to hold us back because of their fears and not for legitimate reasons. Or maybe they're jealous and actually don't want us to succeed."

"Wow, who needs enemies with friends like that?" Nate observed.

"I'd like you to take a few minutes and think about your truly supportive people. Who can you turn to for insight and wisdom? Once you've written those down, we'll look at principle number five."

After the group listed key people I said, "Okay, *Spell out what you'll need to accomplish the goal.* We're talking about skills, time, money or any resources you can foresee needing. Getting back to contacting three companies, how much gas, time and internet research is required before you arrive at their door?"

"And then we get to number six – *Devise an action plan.* All of this pre-work isn't going to help us much if we don't do something. What will you do when? It might look like this: On Monday, I will use three hours to research names of people at these three companies. On Tuesday, I will contact each one and arrange a ten-minute information interview, hopefully for Wednesday or Thursday. I will spend Tuesday afternoon ensuring I have appropriate clothes for the appointment and put gas in my car."

The last step Ziglar emphasized was to – *Note what the benefits to yourself will be upon achieving your goal.* We brainstormed and concluded in our example that visiting three companies could lead immediately to requests for interviews, insights into organizations, increased motivation and self-esteem, and in the long-term to opened doors and material gain.

"So where do you go from here?" I asked.

"Well I'm not exactly sure where I'll end up but at least I'm leaving here with a plan," Lisa announced. "That's more than I've had since I lost my job. Actually, I'm not sure I've ever had a strategic approach to living my life. I've kind of just floated along. I'm excited…and a little bit scared."

## CHANGING COURSE

"It's pretty normal, I think, to experience a range of emotions when you're venturing into new territory. And we are all changed people since you arrived here a month ago, some in obvious ways, and others more subtly, and some in ways that will only be clearer as you begin this next leg of your journey. Our time together has come to an end. Bless you and thank you for working with me, people."

# Conclusion

She chose the spot in the farthest corner of the room and seemed to me a feather – tiny, fragile, like a breeze could pick her up and transport her to another land. Her eyes stayed trained on the floor and her voice, a whisper, was heard only when called on and then with great reluctance. She came to every class, listened respectfully and participated hesitantly in all the group activities. Her name was Maria.

Over four weeks we pieced together Maria's story as facts emerged in class and our one-on-ones. First came a crippling medical diagnosis followed by deteriorating mental health. Her marriage disintegrated and the court awarded full custody of her children to their father. These stresses led to poor job performance and so she was let go. Maria's life as she had known it was gone within two years. The magnitude of the losses overwhelmed her and she curled into a fetal position for over a year. Coming to our program marked Maria's first step back into the world.

Maria completed the program and thanked us for caring about her. On the last day at our celebration lunch she thanked her fellow participants for their support. Then she thanked us instructors and announced that she felt ready to work again. Her confidence grew as she saw herself on paper – a resume and cover letter prepared specifically for her. The interview preparation had shown her how to present her skills in fresh light, and more importantly, she spoke of believing she had something to offer.

And then she added one more comment. "I've been to other programs and courses but something is different about this place. I really felt cared for here. Thank you."

It was enough to know we had planted seeds of care and worth and I prayed they would germinate and blossom. I knew her story would continue long after her encounter with us, but as with the majority of our clients, I believed our part was finished.

The story did not end there.

About four years later she appeared in our office unexpectedly. It was hard to believe that this effervescent woman was the same Maria. Bouncing from hug to hug she gushed her story.

We heard details of her sales and marketing job, a position she had not dared dream of before. She received promotions and bonuses for excellent work. Career-wise she was soaring. She smiled and proudly proclaimed, "I have a life again."

Most client stories did not end this way. Typically people came, rested with us for a while and left, never to return. But enough Maria stories found their way back to us to confirm our belief that changing course within a caring community where people listen, cheer you on and remind you of who you really are *can* make a difference. It is my hope that these pages have been a reminder that you are not alone and will encourage you to both find and be a support to others along this journey.

What will your story be?

# Notes

1. Personal Style Indicator is a self-scored learning and communication instrument published by Consulting Resource Group International. Ideas from this chapter and *I've Got Style* are based on material from the PSI. It is available at: www.crgleader.com
2. Tony Beshara, *Acing the Interview: How to Ask and Answer the Questions That Will Get You the Job*, (New York: Amacom Publishers, 2008).
3. Robert Pryor and Jim Bright, *The Chaos Theory of Careers: A New Perspective on Working in the Twenty-First Century*, (London, UK: Routledge, 2011).
4. Henry Cloud and John Townsend, *Boundaries: When to Say YES, When to Say NO to Take Control of Your Life,* Revised edition, (Grand Rapids, MI: Zondervan, 2002).
5. Stephen R. Covey, A. Roger Merrill, and Rebecca R. Merrill, *First Things First,* (New York: Simon & Schuster, 1995), 88-90.
6. Brene Brown, "BRAVING INVENTORY: Rumbling with Trust," *Courage Works,* http://www.courageworks.com/classes/the-anatomy-of-trust/lessons/the-anatomy-of-trust (accessed January 15, 2016).
7. Zig Ziglar, *See You at the Top,* (Gretna, LA: Pelican Publishing Co., 1975).
8. *Ziglar,* http://www.ziglar.com/about/zig-ziglar-bio (accessed January 12, 2016)

# CHANGING COURSE

Made in the USA
Columbia, SC
17 May 2017